D0915604

Flowers to Philanthropy

THIS BOOK MADE POSSIBLE BY:

COPPERMARK BANK
EXPRESS PERSONNEL SERVICES
ROBERT H. MEINDERS
MERRILL LYNCH—
MEYERS WILLIAMSON GROUP
OKLAHOMA CITY UNIVERSITY

Clayton I. Bennett
Bob Burke
Tom Butler
Luke Corbett
Bob & Nedra Funk
Mo & Jacque Grotjohn
Burns Hargis
Tom & Brenda McDaniel
Steve Moore
Lee Allan Smith
J. Blake Wade

Flowers to Philanthropy

The Life of Herman Meinders

by
Bob Burke and Tom Butler

foreword by
Dr. Robert H. Schuller

series editor
Gini Moore Campbell

associate editors
Eric Dabney and Stephanie Ayala

OKLAHOMA HERITAGE ASSOCIATION
Oklahoma City, Oklahoma

Copyright 2004 by Oklahoma Heritage Association

Printed in the United States of America.
ISBN 1-885596-44-8
Library of Congress Catalog Number 2004114984
Designed by Red Square Design, Inc.

Unless otherwise noted, photographs are courtesy of the Herman and LaDonna Meinders Family.

OKLAHOMA HERITAGE ASSOCIATION
201 Northwest Fourteenth Street
Oklahoma City, Oklahoma 73103

Contents

Acknowledgments

Herman Meinders and flowers have much in common. Henry Ward Beecher wrote, "Flowers have a mysterious and subtle influence upon the feelings." Flowers have the power to calm, to stimulate the imagination, and to awaken memories. Flowers are messengers of love and encouragement.

Anyone who has been around Herman for even a few hours can testify to his uplifting and loving spirit. He is the eternal optimist, like flowers, sending out messages of love and encouragement. Herman is true to the floral tradition of complimenting people and thanking friends for their kindness and consideration.

"Knowing Herman," said his friend, Ray Ackerman, "is like getting a thank you note with a bouquet of roses every day. He always tells me how much good I'm doing—no matter what the occasion." ABC commentator Paul Harvey said, "Flowers make people bloom." So does Herman.

We have many bouquets to send to so many people who helped make this book possible. Herman and his wife, LaDonna, opened their home and office to us to review files and search through boxes and scrapbooks of photographs. LaDonna conducted many of the interviews of people who have played important roles in Herman's life.

Mo Grotjohn, Glennis Wright, Donna Corjay, Evelyn Chappell, Jack Nessen, and Connie Peak helped research the history of the company, provided photographs, and contributed other information

> We thank our series editor, Gini Moore Campbell, and associate editors, Eric Dabney and Stephanie Ayala. Also contributing were Rodger Harris, Bill Welge, Chester Cowen, Judith Michener, and Bill Moore at the Oklahoma Historical Society; Linda Lynn, Melissa Hayer, Mary Phillips, Robin Davison, and Billie Harry at the Oklahoma Publishing Company archives; and Kitty Pittman, Mary Hardin, Adrienne Abrams, Melecia Caruthers, and Marilyn Miller at the Oklahoma Department of Libraries.

> We are also indebted to our team of researchers, photographers, and transcribers—Robert Burke, Amy Nicar, Shelley Dabney, Amy Clakley, and Stephanie Ayala.

> Thanks also to the Oklahoma Heritage Association, and its chairman, Clay Bennett, for continuing to preserve the bold and exciting story of Oklahoma through its publications program.

> Oklahoma's incredible story is not about places and events—it is about our people—like Herman Meinders.

Bob Burke
Tom Butler
2004

Foreword

I first met Herman Meinders when he invited me to speak to a convention of his employees and floral associates in Las Vegas, Nevada. My first impression was that he was a man full of energy and very enthusiastic. His words and actions exposed his integrity—because only people who are truly sincere and honest can be enthusiastic.

Without integrity, Herman could not have built one of the most successful businesses in America. If he had been less than honest with his customers, his subconscious would have built a defense mechanism against enthusiasm, because one's subconscious cannot run the risk of letting the cat out of the bag or exposing a true identity. Without integrity, one lives with secrets. With secrets, one cannot have enthusiasm—it is too dangerous.

Herman has contributed to his community in so many ways. His heart is big and his vision is even larger. Herman has discovered that the key to happiness is the joy of giving.

The longer I have known Herman, the more I believe that my first impression was correct. He is a man of integrity and great generosity. I am honored to call him my friend.

Dr. Robert H. Schuller
Pastor, Author, Motivator
Crystal Cathedral
Garden Grove, California

Herman Meinders Genealogy

WEENER, GERMANY

Harm Meinders   Antje Brouwer Meinders

October 12, 1860-June 18, 1937   November 8, 1865-February 21, 1953

Married 1888

Jan
September 1, 1889-July 20, 1951

Jantje
October 16, 1891-May 7, 1957

Lambertus
August 3, 1894-February 2, 1959

Harm
February 10, 1896-February 24, 1979

Antje
September 5, 1897-October 8, 1957

Hinderina
February 8, 1899-June 11, 1977

Ted
July 11, 1900-March 17, 1959

Hero
(Herman's father who became known as Harold after immigrating to the United States in 1929)
January 11, 1905-June 10, 1972

Carl Buntjer   Gertrude Janssen Buntjer

(Born in Weener, Germany)

March 7, 1874-July 3, 1946   February 9, 1878-January 5, 1930

Married December 30, 1895

John
May 1, 1896-June 6, 1946

William
August 26, 1897-March 27, 1966

Elizabeth
March 15, 1899-August 14, 1985

Grace
September 15, 1900-January 7, 1975

Frances
September 24, 1907-March 13, 1982

(Herman's mother was born in German Valley, Illinois)

Ben
May 27, 1912-October 14, 1979

German Roots

The Herman Meinders story begins in the latter years of the 19th century along the North Sea in far northwestern Germany. In 1888, Herman's grandfather, Harm Meinders, married young Antje Brouwer and settled in the tiny farming village of Holthusen, just one mile from the German border with the Netherlands.

Harm and Antje began their family the following year with a son, Jan. During the next 16 years, seven other children were born to the hard-working farm family—Jantje, Lambertus, Harm, Hinderina, Antje, Ted, and Herman's father, Hero, born January 11, 1905.

Life was simple and often harsh for Harm, Antje, and their eight children who lived in a house attached to a large barn that shielded their small dairy herd from the ravages of the winter wind that swept in from the North Sea. After the cattle were milked each morning, they were walked to a mile-square public grazing area in the city center. At the end of the day, the cattle were herded back to the barn for a second milking.

The Meinders spoke Low German, a division of the German language that developed over the centuries in a narrow fringe along the border between Germany and the Netherlands. Low German contained more slang and informal words than High German, the language of the larger German cities and of German literature.

Hero, the baby of the large family, worked hard on the farm, but often talked with other youth in the village about the direction that Germany was headed. The country had been crushed by its enemies in World War I and its people were living under the rigid terms imposed by the Treaty of Versailles in 1919.

Germany had a new government that was suffocating from a huge war debt and could not possibly pay all that was

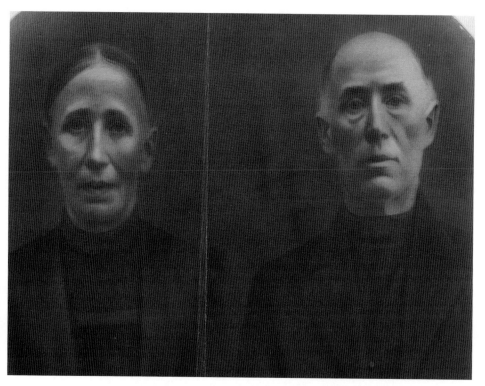

Herman's grandparents, Antje, left, and Harm Meinders, were hard-working farmers in northwestern Germany along the North Sea. They lived out their lives in their homeland.

demanded in reparations. During the 1920s, Germany fell behind in payments to France and other countries. The failing economy caused spiraling inflation that wiped out savings, pensions, insurance, and other forms of fixed income for Germans. The chaos created a social revolution that destabilized the nation and allowed the rise of the Nationalist Socialist (Nazi) German Workers' party, led by Adolf Hitler.

Hero personally saw how inflation was ruining his country. The German mark became so devalued that it took nearly a suitcase full of paper money to buy a loaf of bread.[1]

Hero became a political activist and traveled to Berlin to march in support of the ruling Social Democratic Party that was valiantly trying to hold the parliamentary government together despite both conservatives and socialists hiring private armies in attempts to overthrow the government.

During one march in the Berlin square, Hero and his fellow marchers were greatly intimidated by Hitler's followers. Hero was jabbed with the butt of a rifle swung by a young, screaming Nazi.

The S.S. *Bremen*, the ship which carried Hero Meinders to America in 1929, was built just two years before and operated by The North German Lloyd. This photograph of the ship came from the berthing book published by the ship's owner before it sailed from Germany to the United States.

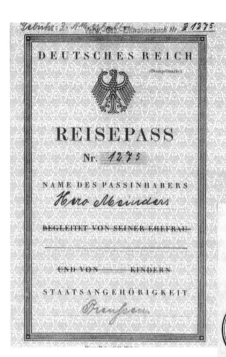

Hero Meinders' German passport issued just four weeks before he left Germany and sailed to New York City in January, 1929. Once he arrived in the United States, officials at Ellis Island changed his name to Harold Meinders.

Hero became increasingly pessimistic about his future in Germany. The uneasiness of the direction of his homeland was amplified by glowing reports of America he received in letters from his older brother, Ted, who had left Germany and settled in Minnesota five years before.[2]

After talking it over with his parents, Hero made plans to visit his brother in America. On January 10, 1929, he boarded the S.S. *Bremen*, a nearly-new German passenger ship operated by The North German Lloyd and under the command of Kapitan Von Thulen. The ship sailed from Bremen, Germany, to New York City, with stops in Southampton, England, and Cherbourg, France.

The waters of the North Sea and the North Atlantic are

usually rough in January—but were especially choppy in January, 1929. Borders had to be installed on the galley tables to prevent dishes from sliding to the floor. Hero was extremely ill for most of the 10-day trip and promised himself that he would not return home to Germany in such a manner.

The brochure handed Hero when he boarded the *Bremen* anticipated sea sickness. In a section titled "Information for Passengers," a new cure was mentioned. The brochure said, "Travelers who have a tendency to suffer from sea-sickness have an opportunity on this steamer to undergo an entirely new treatment whereby there is relief through a process of inhaling certain remedies."[3] The new treatment had no effect upon Hero.

Just after his 24th birthday, Hero arrived with thousands of other immigrants at Ellis Island in New York Harbor. He had little money— he had used most of his cash to purchase passage to America. He did not speak English, although he found many German-speaking people at Ellis Island. The processing center was busy and was accus-

Herman received his middle name, Carl, from his maternal grandfather, Carl Buntjer, who lived in the same town in Germany as the Meinders until he emigrated to the United States.

The family of Herman's mother, Frances Buntjer Meinders. Left to right, back row, Frances and her sisters and brothers, Grace, Bill, John and Elizabeth. Front row, her father Carl Buntjer, brother Ben, and mother Gertrude Buntjer.

tomed to large numbers of German immigrants. In fact, more than 20 million immigrants came through Ellis Island from 1880 to 1930.

The first group of German settlers arrived in the American colonies in 1683 and the flow continued unabated for the next 250 years. As with Hero, most Germans immigrated to America for economic reasons. First came small farmers, followed by craftsmen, cottage industry workers, and day laborers. By 1800, nine percent of the United States population had ties to Germany. The peak of German immigration to the United States was in the 1880s when more than 1.5 million Germans arrived.[4]

At Ellis Island, Hero was welcomed to America and told

that his name would not be accepted in the United States. Immigration officials gave him a new first name—Harold. Because Hero had no middle name, his official documents listed his middle name as "None."

After the processing was completed, Harold used his remaining money to purchase a train ticket for passage to Flandreau, South Dakota, where his brother, Ted, had moved to work on a farm. Harold was amazed at the variety and beauty of the American countryside as he left New York City and saw huge barns and thousands of cattle hovered around stacks of hay in Pennsylvania.

There were other German immigrants headed westward. By 1929, many Germans had followed the migration of America west, with large numbers settling in the Midwestern states of Ohio, Indiana, Illinois, Missouri, Michigan, Wisconsin, Iowa, Nebraska, North Dakota, South Dakota, and Minnesota.[5] Like other immigrant groups, the Germans tended to settle near family members and friends who were already established in America.

Harold arrived in Flandreau, only a few miles west of the South Dakota-Minnesota line. Because Ted was operating a small farm, there was no additional work there for Harold. However, he was able to find a job on a larger dairy farm owned by the Janson family. Mrs. Janson was a schoolteacher who spoke excellent English.

Harold recognized he was handicapped by only speaking German, although most of his friends and acquaintances lived in the German farm settlements around Flandreau. He asked Mrs. Janson to teach him English. The informal lessons were completed in an unusual setting—each morning and evening, while Mrs. Janson and Harold were milking cows, they practiced translation from German to English. Although Harold's English was broken, at best, he was able to communicate with English-speaking citizens in the area.[6]

With increased confidence gained by elimination of the language barrier, Harold took advantage of an opportunity to go into business for himself in 1932 in nearby Pipestone, Minnesota.

Pipestone, the county seat of Pipestone County, was founded in 1876 by Charles Bennett and Daniel Sweet, who were intrigued by the nearby quarries made famous in a poem, "The Song of Hiawatha," by Henry Wadsworth Longfellow. The Pipestone Quarries contained large deposits of soft pipestone that had been used by Native Americans for thousands of years to fashion ceremonial pipes and other items. Many tribes— Ojibwa, Dakota, Oto, Pawnee, Sac, Fox, and Lakota—came to quarry the sacred redstone known as pipestone and catlinite. The pipestone became a valuable trade item and was responsible for Pipestone becoming a crossroads of the Indian world.[7]

By the 1930s, Pipestone had become a major travel and business center in southwest Minnesota. Decades of boomtown status in the late 1800s resulted in the construction of many buildings in downtown Pipestone. The area is now the Pipestone Historic District.[8]

With a loan from friends, Harold purchased a used truck with a feed grinder mounted on the back. Harold believed corn growers in the area would pay for grinding services that could be provided on their property. The mobile feed grinder saved farmers the trouble and expense of hauling their harvested corn miles to a feed mill.

Harold's idea worked. Soon he was busy from daylight to dark, traveling from farm to farm. His grinder ground corn that was taken directly from the fields into nourishing cattle feed—the corn cobs gave the feed bulk. The only negative aspect of the feed grinding business was Harold's constant exposure to dust, an exposure that would later limit his ability to work and shorten his life.

Almost immediately, Harold's enterprise became successful. Soon he added another truck and feed grinder, a truck to hull oats, and two drivers to help him. He saved enough money from earnings to pay cash for the new equipment.

In the summer of 1931, Harold met Frances Buntjer, a German girl who was visiting her sister in Flandreau. Frances was born in German Valley, Illinois, on September 24, 1907, but her parents, Carl and Gertrude Janssen Buntjer, had come to America from the same town in Germany where the Meinders had lived.

When Harold and Frances Meinders were married on November 25, 1936, they moved into a two-story frame house on West Main Street in Pipestone.

It was indeed a small world. Frances and Harold liked each other very much—they both spoke Low German, loved the same types of food, and enjoyed German music. They fell in love and talked about marriage. It was a long distance relationship for awhile because Frances went home to Munich, North Dakota, where her family had moved when she was small. Soon, Harold asked Frances to marry him—she said yes.[9]

Harold decided to make the long trip to North Dakota to consummate his marriage plans, but his only transportation was a feed-grinding truck, certainly less than romantic transportation. However, his friend, Glen "Ike" Eichhorn, loaned Harold his 1934 Ford. Eichhorn owned a used car lot adjacent to an automobile service station where he helped the owner during the lunch hour. It was at the station that Eichhorn met Harold when he was refueling his grain grinder truck.[10]

The trip to North Dakota was a success. Harold and Frances were married in Egeland, North Dakota, on November 25, 1936, and returned to Pipestone to begin their life together.

Harold continued his grinding business and Frances set up housekeeping in a two-story frame house in town.[11]

Harold and Frances were married at the height of the Great Depression, the worst and longest period of high unem-

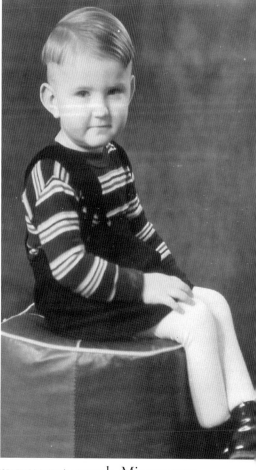

Herman Carl Meinders was born in Pipestone, Minnesota, on November 15, 1937, the first of five children of Harold and Frances Meinders.

ployment and low business activity in modern history. The Depression had begun in October, 1929, with the crash of the stock market in New York City, just nine months after Harold arrived in the United States. It worsened as banks failed, stores and factories closed, and millions of Americans were left jobless and homeless.

Minnesota farms were hit hard by the Depression. With low prices for crops, many farmers faced bankruptcy. Often Harold waited months for payment for grain-grinding services.

As if the sour economy were not enough, Minnesotans endured several consecutive years of drought. One of Harold's neighbors, Arnold Janson, remembered the day that townspeople ran into the streets to look at an approaching dark cloud. One man said, "It's gonna' rain! I know it's gonna' rain!" Unfortunately, the cloud was nothing more than millions of grasshoppers that had attacked another nearby grain field.[1][2]

Just before their first anniversary, Frances gave birth to their first child, Herman Carl Meinders, on November 15, 1937. Although the young couple was overjoyed with the new baby, Harold knew the additional mouth to feed would strain a family budget that was already tight because of the ravages of the Great Depression.

Chores, Chores and More Chores

CHAPTER 2

HERMAN WORKED SO HARD ON THE FARM, THERE WAS
NO TIME LEFT FOR SCHOOL OR COMMUNITY ACTIVITIES.
JACK NESSEN

Herman spoke German for the first four years of his life. Then, America entered World War II and German-Americans were sometimes harassed and treated unfairly because the Third Reich had become one of America's principal enemies. The Meinders family in Minnesota did not escape such discrimination.

A neighbor told Harold Meinders, "If your boy doesn't stop talking German, they will take you away to a camp for the rest of the war." That insinuation caused English to be the only language spoken in the home. Harold and Frances worked with Herman's teacher at Pipestone Elementary School to make

Herman's mother, Frances Meinders, always dressed Herman in his finest clothes for Sunday school at the Lutheran church in Pipestone, Minnesota.

certain he learned and spoke good English.[1]

Early in Herman's school years, the Meinders family purchased and moved to a 50-acre farm one mile south of downtown Pipestone. There was no indoor plumbing in the old house on the property. It was a drab existence for the young family that knew nothing but long, hard days of work and tight budgets.

Harold was proud of his German ancestry and kept in touch with his family in the old country. He disliked Hitler as much as any other American, especially because Hitler's domination of Germany had been a primary reason Harold had not returned home after his 1929 visit to Minnesota and South Dakota. Harold spoke broken English even into the middle years of his adult life. He was a stern disciplinarian and hard worker who was always ready to help his neighbors in time of trouble. However, the extensive exposure to dust in grinding corn eventually caught up with Harold. Emphysema disabled him by 1946.

Herman's mother, Frances, spoke excellent English. She had grown up in America and helped Herman with his school lessons, especially his transition to speaking English. Frances was

Right: Herman at age two with his parents, Harold and Frances Meinders. The elder Meinders was a hard-working farmer and grain grinder and Frances ran a sharp, German household. *Below:* Herman at age 11 in 1948. He was old enough to take on many respon-sibilities around the family farm, both before and after school.

an incredible German cook and helped a great deal on the farm.

At an early age, Herman was given chores to perform around the Meinders farm and home. He quickly grew to be tall and skinny—he could work as hard as many adults in the backbreaking la-bor associated with a dairy farm. As the eldest child, Herman helped his parents take care of his brothers and sisters as the Meinders family grew. Donna Mae was born January 1, 1941;

Donald Gene was born May 11, 1942; Robert Harold was born July 14, 1945; and Linda Ann was born August 30, 1951. All five Meinders children were born in Pipestone.[2]

The family arose at 6:00 a.m., an hour before dawn in the winter, and milked the herd of dairy cattle that ranged from eight to twelve. When his younger siblings were still too small to help, Herman and his parents milked the cows. While the milk was separating, Frances went into the house and prepared breakfast—most often it consisted of bacon and eggs, oatmeal, and homemade German white or black bread.

Herman walked a mile to school each morning. The bell rang at 8:00 a.m., so at times he left his house at 7:00 a.m. in the winter to trudge through snow banks to the school building in Pipestone that held classes for all 13 grades, including kindergarten. Herman was attentive to his teachers, but was shy and did not enjoy being called upon to recite in class.

George Schulze, later Pipestone's leading florist, was Herman's classmate and attended the same church, St. Paul Lutheran Church. Schulze never understood why Herman was so skinny—his friends called him Ichabod—because Herman's mother

Harold and Frances Meinders in 1961.

Left: Everyone in the Meinders family pitched in to complete chores both in the home and on the farm. Left to right, back row, Bob, Don, Herman, and Donna. Front row, mother Frances, sister Linda, and father Harold Meinders.

Right: Herman, left, and his little sister, Linda. Herman was kind to his sisters and always brought them gifts after he left for college and returned home for visits.

made the best homemade bread in town.[3]

After school, Herman walked home and began a long list of chores. He fed pigs and chickens, fed calves with pails of milk, and milked the cows a second time each day. In the winter, it was quite an operation to provide fresh water for the animals. Water in a large tank was frozen by temperatures that often dropped to 30 degrees below zero. To thaw the water, Herman fed corn cobs, and occasionally

Left: Herman was 16 years old when he purchased his first car, a 1940 Chevrolet. The front seat of the car had to be large to accommodate his long legs.

Right: Harold Meinders bought his first tractor in February, 1948. Tractors were difficult to acquire after World War II rationing, but he was able to purchase the tractor after obtaining a contract to mow the Pipestone Municipal Airport.

a few pieces of coal, into a heater in the center of the tank. The resulting warmth thawed the water, necessary to keep the cattle and other farm animals alive.[4]

Herman's pigs were well fed. His father made a deal with the frugal owner of the Pan O' Gold Bakery in Pipestone to buy stale bread for feed. When a load of old bread was available, Herman pulled a four-wheel trailer mounted with a steel box to the rear of the bakery. The baker asked Herman to cover the bread

Left to right, Harold Meinders, and his children Herman, Linda holding the family cat, Don, Bob, and Donna.

with a canvas so townspeople could not see what he was hauling back to the Meinders farm. Often, before Herman or his father took the load of bread home, they stopped at Glen Eichorn's body shop and allowed Glen and his hired hand to choose the freshest of the stale bread.[5]

The Meinders children took turns watching the family cows that were allowed to graze in the fields after hay was cut each summer. Herman's sister, Donna, remembered, "After the hay was cut, Dad would let the cows feed on the leftover hay. Our big responsibility was to keep a close eye on the cattle to make certain they did not stray into the cornfield."[6] To pass the time, Herman once carved a heart out of pipestone from the nearby quarry.

Getting the cattle into the pasture was no easy chore. One huge, white cow had a mind of her own and would try to lead other members of the herd astray as Herman and his siblings used their dog, Spotty, to guide the cows across the highway and a set of railroad tracks to the pasture.[7]

In his teenage years, Herman also worked for his neighbor, Pearl Bemke, who owned a horse barn. On Tuesdays and Thursdays, Herman cleaned out the barn and hauled the manure to a large pile that would be spread on the fields the next spring.

During his years at home, Herman spent so much time with pigs and chickens he developed a lifelong dislike for the animals and swore to himself he would never own any of them in his adult life.

Herman went through confirmation ceremonies at St. Paul Lutheran Church in Pipestone. Herman is third from left on the third row. At top center is the church's pastor, The Reverend Steinmeyer.

The harsh Minnesota winter provided excellent opportunities for families to grow closer. Herman played cards almost every night with his parents, brothers, and sisters. Thanksgiving and Christmas dinners with his aunts, uncles, and cousins became a tradition.

The piles of Minnesota snow provided both fun and hazardous times for Herman and his family. Once, Herman had to rescue his sister, Donna, from a snow bank she had fallen into on the way to school. After Donna thawed out, she and her playmates were back outside tunneling through the deep banks of snow that covered fences. Occasionally, Herman would take time from his chores to help Donna pack snow into blocks to build an ice house.[8]

Herman's father expected hard work from him. One day in the fourth grade, Herman was kept for detention after school for an incident involving his friend, Jack Nessen. Nessen threw a spitball at another student and was caught in the act by the teacher, Inez Clarksean, who asked, "Does anyone think that is funny?" When Herman raised his hand and said, "Yes, I think that was funny!" the result was detention. However, when Herman did not appear at home at the appointed hour to begin his chores, his father came to school looking for him. Harold informed the teacher that Herman was needed every afternoon at home and should never be kept after school again.[9]

The spit ball incident was a turning point in Herman's life. Nessen, who remained Herman's best friend for life, remembered, "Before that day, Herman never said anything out loud. He was quiet and reserved."[10]

A brief respite for Herman from daily hard work on the farm was when he tried out for the Pipestone Junior High School wrestling team. He wrestled at 106 pounds and was quite successful in his first few matches because his exceptional height prevented him from being easily taken down. Herman carried a bottle of honey that he ate before matches to give him strength. But after a few times of missing chores, Herman was forced by his father to give up wrestling and return to his duties with the pigs, chickens, and cattle.[11]

When Herman was in the seventh grade, he tried to train his hair by applying various gels. However, there was a certain section of his hair that would not lie down and stuck straight out from the back of his head. One day in art class, the teacher asked students to cut out a silhouette of some other student. At the end of class, the teacher intended to hold up the silhouettes and allow students to guess their identity.

Most of the class members turned in a silhouette of Herman, with the large tuft of hair sticking out at an odd angle. Students quickly identified the jagged hair profile as that of Herman. Jack Nessen said the profile looked like the old Pontiac Indian emblem.[12]

Another break from farm work came when Herman took a job at the J.C. Penney store in Pipestone during his senior year

Herman's first time card from the J.C. Penney store in Pipestone, Minnesota, showed he received 60 cents an hour. The 47-cent deduction was for F.O.A.B., the old age pension program that predated Social Security retirement.

in high school. He worked at the store after school from 3:30 to 6:00 p.m. on weekdays and all day Saturday. He primarily was a salesman but also swept floors, stocked shelves, and made sale signs in the basement using block letters and an ink roller.

Herman had to dress up for his job at the J.C. Penney store—he wore a shirt and tie most days. However, he was thrilled not to wear a bow tie like his good friend, George Schulze, who worked across the street at the Red Owl grocery store.[13]

J.C. Penney store manager Walt Hughes, and especially assistant manager, Ron Risch, played an important role in training young Herman for a life in business. Herman considered Risch his mentor. Risch was a funny, likeable man who knew when to have fun with his employees and when to be serious and take care of customers and the business side of running the store.[14]

Risch encouraged Herman to work his way up to become a manager of a J.C. Penney store. He gave Herman materials to read about managing a retail store and taught him how to order shoes, shirts, and other dry goods. "Herman was a natural born salesman," lifelong friend Denny Crook said, "He liked people and simply enjoyed telling them about a new kind of product on sale at the store."[15]

Herman was frugal with his 60 cent-per-hour job at J.C. Penney, except during football season. One of his co-workers put together a weekly pool on the Pipestone Arrows football game. Herman really had no idea how the pool worked, but contributed 50 cents to the effort. He was shocked when he received $5.00 for winning the pool the first week of the season. He remembered, "I won three weeks in a row and never had any idea how I was winning!"[16]

Herman learned the intricacies of the shoe business from LeRoy Stueven, the J.C. Penney shoe department manager. Stueven provided a much-needed alibi after Herman wrecked his 1940 light green Chevrolet on the way back to work from home one winter Saturday. Herman, who liked to gun his car so fast that he spun around at a street corner, lost control and slammed into an electric pole. He was worried that his father "would kill him," when he saw the damaged bumper and hood.

Stueven liked to move Herman's car from the back of the J.C. Penney store to the front near closing time because the car had a wolf whistle he enjoyed playing. On the day of Herman's accident, Stueven went to move Herman's car and frantically ran back inside the store, shouting, "Herman, somebody has run into your car." Herman looked at the damage and calmly said, "Oh, boy, can you believe that? How can it be?"

After notifying local police, Herman and Stueven resolved that the culprit would probably never be found. Stueven thought surely some farmer backed into Herman's car with his truck, especially because wood from the electric pole was imbedded in the fender. The following Monday, in daylight, Stueven re-examined the car and concluded that the dent was in the shape of a pole and that the wood fragments were from a utility pole.

He said, "Herman, you hit a pole." But Herman never admitted it to his father.[17]

Herman was responsible for ringing out the cash registers at the J.C. Penney store each night. After the employee responsible for a certain register closed it for the day, Herman delivered the register totals to the cashier.

During pheasant season, the men in the J.C. Penney store took turns hunting during long lunch hours. Too much anticipation to leave the store for the nearby pheasant hunting fields taught Herman a valuable lesson one day. Ron Risch and LeRoy Stueven went hunting at noon and promised Herman they would return at 1:30 p.m. and allow him to hunt for a while. However, at 1:20 p.m., a farmer came into the store wanting to buy a suit.

Herman measured the customer for a suit and helped him pick out a shirt and tie. As Herman nervously watched the clock, the man decided his son should also have a new suit, and the lengthy measuring and selection process began anew. Finally, Herman rang up the sale at his register and ran from the store to go hunting.

That night, when Herman checked the registers, he was $80 short. He counted the cash bag 10 times and reported the shortage to the cashier in the store's upstairs office. She said, "Well, what did you do with it?" Herman was sick to his stomach—the $80 was like $10,000 today. Three or four days later, manager Walt Hughes informed Herman he had picked up the $80 that Herman had failed to take from the counter and place into the register. In the future, Herman made certain the customer's money was in the register before he closed the cash drawer.[18]

At the end of his junior year, Herman and fellow classmates at Pipestone High School were scheduled to take their final examinations. Their first exam was over at 10:00 a.m. and Herman and his friends had nothing but time on their hands before a statewide bookkeeping proficiency exam scheduled for 1:00 p.m.

Herman certainly did not want to go home to do chores, so he and his friends drove to Holland, a small community about nine miles from Pipestone. They bought a gallon of Mogen David wine at a local liquor store and headed for the Pipestone National Monument to swim and drink. Herman drank so much of the wine on the way to the swimming hole, he fell into the creek and ruined his clothes for the day.[19]

When Herman returned to school, looking disheveled, at best, the teacher, Mr. Figge, at first refused Herman's attempt to take the bookkeeping test. Finally, however, the teacher allowed Herman to sit alone at the front of the room, segregated from other students. Although he was suffering from one of the worst headaches of his life, Herman whizzed through the test, thinking surely he had answered questions too quickly and failed. He even waited to leave until other students began leaving.

Miraculously, Herman posted the tenth best score in Minnesota, prompting the teacher to apologize three times for his actions.

Herman's graduation photo in 1955. He stayed in Pipestone for a year
before leaving for college.

Following Jack

CHAPTER 3

IF YOU ARE GOING TO GET AHEAD IN LIFE, YOU REALLY NEED TO GO TO COLLEGE.
RON RISCH

Herman graduated from Pipestone High School in May, 1955, and had no plans to attend college. His father's opinion was that his sons needed no more than a ninth grade education to succeed in life. Herman had been given more responsibility at the Pipestone J.C. Penney store and fully intended to enter a training program to become a store manager. He worked at the store for an entire year after high school graduation.

Herman considered joining four of his friends and enlist in the United States Navy. A recruiter in Sioux Falls, South Dakota, took one look at the skinny Herman and predicted he would not pass the Navy physical examination, although he would allow him to try. Herman, at 6 feet two inches and 136 pounds, and with a mild case of asthma, proved the recruiter correct and failed the physical. His four friends passed, and began Navy training.[1]

Although J.C. Penney assistant store manager Ron Risch

enjoyed training Herman, he was aware of trends in the giant retailer's employment policies—especially the move toward hiring only college graduates as store managers. Risch advised Herman that if he wanted to become a manager of a J.C. Penney store, he would need a college degree.[2]

Herman's best friend, Jack Nessen, had left for college immediately after high school. In his senior year, Nessen had received catalogs from nearly 300 colleges from California to

Herman's graduating class of 1955 at Pipestone High School held a reunion in July of 1995. First row, left to right, Glen Rickerman, George Schulze, Herb Hess, Clarence Taylor, Herman, Darlene Engbarth Wheeler, Eleanor Hulzebos Klostergaard, and Bob Dahl. Second row, Curt Roesler, Charlotte Luttmers Sevlie, Diane Christensen Melrose, Janice Johnson Swanson, Thelma VanderWal Lorezen, Geraldine Haupert Voss, Donna Stueven Mielke, Rhoda Thoreson Becklund, Mary Thies Hargens, and Jeanette Weinkauf Laesecke. Third row, Ken Pape, Sharon Mahoney Nelson, Dee Anna Daugherty Dorsey, Donna Bruns Voss, Mary Lorang Thoelke, Rita Timmer Lear, Norma Beyers Koos, Frank Drenth, Don Hoogland, Spud Leroy Vockrodt, and Gordon Huebner. Fourth row, Bob Mattin, Chuck Wilson, Dale Johannsen, Jim Trageser, Dave Cunningham, Jack Thomas, Orville Slinger, Jerome Pierret, Sylvia Miller Grubb, and Larry Monke. Fifth row, Ronald Sedlacek, Jack Nessen, Ron Francis, Denny Crook, Jim Ross, Janice Freese Converse, Cliff Martens, Royal Lear, Jerry Beadle, Don Roscoe, Marlin Thompson, and Howard Wathen.

New York. He knew he would have to work to put himself through college, and focused on schools that seemed to encourage working students. He settled on Oklahoma City University (OCU), a private Methodist university in Oklahoma's capital city.

OCU began classes in 1904 as Epworth University. The school was the dream of Anton H. Classen, a young lawyer in Edmond, Oklahoma Territory, who made the Land Run of 1889 and used his influence to convince the territorial legislature to establish a teachers' training school that eventually became the University of Central Oklahoma.

Epworth University became Oklahoma City University in 1923. Classen was most famous for establishing a street car line in Oklahoma City, but admittedly his proudest accomplishment in life was a Methodist institution of higher learning for Oklahoma.[3]

Nessen arrived in Oklahoma City, quickly found a job as a billing clerk at Chief Freightlines, and joined the Lambda Chi Alpha fraternity. After successfully going through rush, he moved into the fraternity house adjacent to the OCU campus.

Nessen frequently communicated with Herman by letter. Herman was the only one of his close friends in high school who did not attend college, so Nessen's letters contained great detail of college life, including parties and the beautiful girls he had found in warm Oklahoma. In one letter, he told Herman that the winter time temperatures in Oklahoma had to be 40 degrees warmer that in snow-covered Minnesota. Nessen was also excited that he had instantly found a host of new friends by moving into the fraternity house.[4]

In early 1956, Herman decided he wanted to take a look at OCU. His letters to Nessen asked if he could bring his aquarium to the fraternity house. Herman had invested a few of his hard earned dollars in guppies and mollys, tropical fish he placed in the hollowed-out portion of an old car battery.[5]

To make a decision to attend college at OCU, Herman had to talk to two people—his father and Ron Risch. Risch was excited and promised to help Herman transfer to a J.C. Penney store in Oklahoma City. Herman's father was less than enthusiastic about Herman attending college, but agreed to accompany his son to Oklahoma City for a brief weekend visit in February, 1956.

January, 1956 in Pipestone was bitter cold with morning lows dropping to 20 to 25 degrees below zero. On the night before they left for Oklahoma City, Herman told his father, "If it's colder than 20 below zero tomorrow morning, I will never spend another winter in Minnesota." Before the Meinders warmed up their car and headed south toward Oklahoma City, they

Above: Herman's family in1959. Left to right, front row, Donna, Harold, Frances, and Linda. Back row, Don, Herman, and Bob. *Left:* The Meinders siblings in 1987. Left to right, Donna, Herman, Don, Linda, and Bob.

checked the thermometer on the back porch. It was 33 degrees below zero![6]

Even though Herman had only a few hours to look over the OCU campus, he liked what he saw. He was impressed with Nessen's group of friends at the fraternity house. Herman's father was impressed with the 50-degree change in temperature and the

Carl Brandt was Herman's Lambda Chi Alpha "big brother." Herman admired Brandt and the two remained friends following college.

green fields of winter wheat he saw across northern Oklahoma.

In early summer, Herman moved to Oklahoma City and began work in the shoe department of the J.C. Penney store at the Mayfair Shopping Center at Northwest 50th Street and May Avenue, earning $1.00 per hour. He moved into Nessen's spacious room in a rooming house on Northwest 25th Street near the OCU campus.

Herman declared business as his college major and enrolled in a salesmanship class in summer school. Many OCU students worked fulltime jobs, so the university administration created work-friendly class schedules. Herman's classes were early in the morning, giving him ample opportunity to work most of the day at the J.C. Penney store, which was open until 9:00 p.m. Herman always worked at least 40 hours a week while attending college.[7]

Herman's first college professor was a retired military man who promised his tests would cover only material discussed during class time. However, when Herman discovered that many of the questions on the first exam were not from material in the textbook or in his class notes, he confronted the professor. Herman sheepishly learned that the class met for three hours each day, with a short break in the middle. Herman, whose only classroom experience was in one-hour periods in high school, had been leaving at the intermission and had no idea that he was missing the second half of each day's lecture.

There was no doubt that Herman had become an expert on shoes. That ability was apparent one night when he noticed that Nessen's shoes did not match. For nearly a year, Nessen had proudly worn his black dress shoes with his tuxedo to dozens of fraternity parties and dances. When he asked Herman, "Why do you think only one of my shoes has a round arch in the bottom?" Herman began laughing.

It was apparent that one shoe had two eyelets and was wing-tipped—the other shoe had a smooth toe and had three eyelets. The shoes were even different sizes. Herman laughed into the night. The longer Herman laughed, the angrier Nessen became toward the shoe salesman at Bond's Department Store who had sold him the obviously different shoes he had worn for more than a year.[8]

At the beginning of the fall semester, Herman was uncertain about joining Nessen's fraternity and moved into ancient barracks that were serving as a men's dormitory on the OCU campus. Within a few days, however, Nessen and his friends convinced Herman to pledge the fraternity and move into the three-story house at 2323 North Indiana Avenue, near the campus. Herman did not need much encouragement because a fellow student from Alaska kept everyone in the dormitory up all night with his loud partying.[9]

The nine months in the Lambda Chi house were an incredibly happy time for Herman, who roomed with Donald Ford, a ministerial student from Tulsa, Oklahoma. Their room was in the northeast corner of the top floor, just down the hallway from Nessen. Herman especially liked the fraternity pet, a dog named "Damn it." Eyebrows of passersby were often raised when one of the fraternity members yelled from the front door of the house, "Here, Damn it, here Damn it!" The only person who would not call the Boxer by his real name was house cook Mary Padilla. When she was shooing the dog from the kitchen, she was often overheard saying, "Get out of here, Butch."[10]

Herman worked 40 hours a week at J.C. Penney and spent most of his free time performing the duties of a fraternity pledge. The first semester, he carried 13 hours and made mostly

Cs. To try to improve his grades, he enrolled in only nine hours the second semester, but his academic performance did not improve.[11]

It had been a rough winter in Oklahoma City. As a favor one morning, Jack Nessen volunteered to chop the ice from Herman's windshield. Unfortunately, the hatchet he used cut too deeply and scratched the windshield.

Nessen decided the weather in Oklahoma was getting colder, and he wanted an even warmer climate. For some reason, long ago forgotten, he talked to his father about attending the University of Georgia. Nessen's wise father said, "If you're going for the warm weather, why not go all the way to Florida?" Nessen agreed and settled on Florida Southern University (FSU) in Lakeland, Florida, east of Tampa.[12]

Disenchanted with his less than great performance in the classroom, Herman decided to follow his best friend, Nessen, to FSU.

After a brief visit with his parents in Minnesota, Herman and Nessen drove their cars to Lakeland, enrolled in FSU, and Herman moved into a dormitory while frantically looking for a job. He had no money and knew he must earn good money quickly to be able to pay tuition and room and board at the

Herman poses at the Georgia boundary on his way to Florida in 1957. *Courtesy Jack Nessen.*

Lambda Chi fraternity house where Nessen lived.[13]

Unfortunately, thousands of other college students and Northerners had been lured by the Florida climate and jobs in Lakeland were non-existent. Unable to find a job, Herman could not pay his tuition bill and dropped out of classes. He also had no money to pay his housing bill. He continued to eat at the dormitory cafeteria because the lady who checked identification cards recognized him from previous weeks and fortuitously did not ask to see his student ID card.

Herman moved his job search to nearby Tampa. One Saturday morning, he stopped at a Gulf Supermarket on Hillsboro Street and asked the manager if the store had any job openings. The manager said, "Well, our bag boy didn't show up today, so if you want, you can carry out groceries for customers."[14]

There was no guaranteed pay being a bag boy, but Herman made the best of it and thankful customers paid him a total of $3.50 for the day's work. Herman was elated and thought he surely had found solid employment in Tampa. But on Monday morning, when he showed up at the store early, the manager told him weekdays were slow and the store did not need anyone to bag and carry out groceries.

At about the time the manager was preparing to send Herman on his way, the store received a call that the young man who sorted and cased soft drink bottles for company salesmen would be absent that day. Herman jumped at the opportunity, and in record time, organized the bottles and won the heart of the store manager, Melvin Childers, a "country boy" from North Carolina.[15]

Soon Herman was placed in charge of the Gulf Supermarket dairy department, where he found sour milk smells emanating from the dairy cases. With a bucket of water and rags, he cleaned the cases and displayed milk and other dairy items in neat rows. When the Borden salesman was unhappy that Herman had cut back the number of rows for bottles of his brand, he enticed Herman to increase the Borden allocation by giving the young dairy department employee a Pecan Roll.[16]

Herman did such a good job in the dairy department that he quickly was given responsibility for buying frozen food and eggs for all nine Gulf stores in the area. He even bought a truckload of fresh eggs from the Fecker Company in his hometown of Pipestone.

Under the tutelage of the store manager, Herman learned a lot about marketing. He found that if he priced margarine for 20 cents a pound, a customer only bought a pound. However, if the margarine was advertised for "5 pounds for a dollar, limit 5," customers often bought 5 pounds of the product.[17]

Herman became so friendly with the store manager that Childers told him to call him "Mel," a privilege given only a handful of store employees. When another employee addressed Childers as Mel, he was reprimanded.

The grocery store business was a wonderful learning ground for Herman. He got along fine with salesmen who would go out of their way to give him a good deal on a new product. Once when the Kraft salesman convinced Herman to buy 65 cases of Kraft's new Miracle Whip margarine, Herman had to ask permission to use part of the meat market freezer for storage. The meat market manager threw a huge fit and took his complaints all the way to the president of Gulf Supermarkets. By the time the president arrived, Herman had sold most of the margarine, although to appease the meat market manager, Herman had to sell 15 cases of the margarine to other Gulf stores.[18]

The Miracle Whip incident taught Herman valuable marketing lessons. He learned to properly display products and to take advantage of national and local advertising by manufacturers. He sold the new margarine quickly because his customers were learning about the product on radio and television and in newspapers.

Herman lived in a tiny apartment owned by a florist within three blocks of the supermarket. He paid $15 a week for the accommodations.

Just before Christmas of 1957, Herman, age 20, and store manager Childers began talking about opening a restaurant together. Childers knew how to add cereal to hamburger meat to increase profits on hamburgers, and how to calculate profits on wine and alcoholic beverages. They began looking for an establishment they could buy and operate. What they found was Sammy's Bar.

Sammy's Bar

CHAPTER 4

I'LL LOAN YOU THE $1,500 AS LONG AS YOU'RE
NOT GONNA' USE IT FOR SCHOOL.
HAROLD MEINDERS

Sammy's Bar was in a poor section of Tampa on Florida Avenue where three distinctively different low income neighborhoods of whites, Hispanics, and blacks converged. However, Herman and Childers believed they could turn a profit in the bar if they served good food and opened from 7:00 a.m. to 1:00 a.m. The purchase price of the bar was $3,000—but there was no way Herman could come up with his half of the price unless he asked for a loan from his father. He wrote his father about his idea and how he had figured out how many more glasses of beer he could get from a keg if he used eight-ounce glasses rather than nine-ounce glasses.[1]

Harold Meinders owned a commercial building in downtown Pipestone that contained a profitable bar, the Blue Moon, operated by Wes Sedlacek, so he liked the idea of his son buying into such a similar business in Florida. However, echoing his past advice that a college education was unnecessary, Harold

44 / HERMAN MEINDERS

told his son, "OK, I'll loan you the $1,500 as long as you're not gonna' use it for school." Herman agreed.[2]

The only hang-up in negotiations to buy the bar was the seller's insistence that he keep the business until after he could host a huge New Year's Eve party for his friends and customers. Herman and Childers refused to delay the sale, knowing that the New Year's Eve trade at the bar would be a great way to start the business successfully.[3]

A major problem Herman did not anticipate in the bar business was his age. When he went to Tampa city offices to obtain his license to run the bar, he discovered one had to be 21 to obtain a license—Herman was 20 and devastated. He had just bought a bar that he could not legally work in. However, his best friend, Jack Nessen, came to the rescue.

Nessen was still going to college at Florida Southern University and came to Tampa to visit Herman. "You need a phony ID," was Nessen's sure fire answer to Herman's dilemma. Nessen had joined the Army National Guard and, as a company clerk, had access to blank military passes. He dressed Herman in a national guard uniform and took him to a photo booth at a nearby carnival to make the "official" photo for an identification card. The photo and information making Herman 21 was pasted onto a piece of paper that was laminated by an elderly lady whose lawn was graced with a sign that read, "Notary Public and We Laminate Things."[4]

There was another problem. City officials accepted the phony ID but wanted some official proof of Herman's date of birth and lack of criminal record. Herman had to think quickly because he knew Tampa officials would check the birth records at the courthouse in Pipestone. It occurred to Herman that his former next door neighbor, Marion Noble, was the county clerk of Pipestone County, so Herman called her.

Herman told the county clerk, "I'm applying for this deal and I have to prove my date of birth and that I don't have a criminal record. I have to be 21 but I'm only 20. Can you help me out?" Noble, who had always been impressed with Herman's work ethic, agreed, never knowing exactly why she was changing the date of Herman's birth.[5]

The bar business was sour from the beginning. The band that Herman hired for New Year's Eve was so bad that one customer pulled his switchblade and threatened to kill members of the band if they continued playing. Appropriately frightened, the three band members left the bar and hid in the cold alley while Herman began giving the irate customer free drinks until he passed out. Only then did Herman allow the band to come back inside and resume its "concert."[6]

It was the coldest January in Tampa in decades. Very few Northerners came to Tampa, and locals stayed at home and did not frequent Sammy's Bar. With not enough income to pay utilities, Herman looked for other jobs while waiting for the bar to succeed. He tried to sell Niagara massage machines and heating pads, but could not come up with sufficient money to buy sample units. He took a job selling pots and pans door to door. However, when a father became enraged at the salesman who was training Herman because his daughter had bought the cooking set while he was at work, Herman thought, "I don't want to spend my days convincing girls to buy pans so they can get a free hope chest."[7]

To earn extra money, Herman moved his living quarters to an entire floor of a building across the street from the bar. He reserved for himself a tiny room in the back but threw mattresses on the floor in the halls and in other rooms for a mini-hotel business. When customers at the bar over-imbibed, Herman rented them a place to sleep it off for 50 cents a night.[8]

Herman and his partner valiantly tried to succeed in their venture. They had a shuffleboard table, a bumper pool table, and a jukebox. But Herman recognized it was only a matter of time until he and Childers would be forced to close the bar. Herman needed a job.

In a moment of incredible fate, a man named Dale Murphy came into the bar one Saturday evening. Murphy had randomly picked a motel in Tampa and Sammy's Bar happened to be the nearest bar. Murphy, a salesman for the National Florist Directory (NFD) of Leachville, Arkansas, was wearing a suit when he walked into the bar. It was the only time anyone in a suit had entered the bar, so Herman took note when Murphy

Dale Murphy was a salesman for the National Florist Directory who introduced Herman to the floral industry. The fateful invitation came at Sammy's Bar on a slow Saturday night.

announced, "I want a beer and want to shoot some shuffleboard." Herman had become proficient at shuffleboard and entertained his customer with a competitive game. Murphy was having so much fun that he kept drinking glasses of beer and soon wanted to play pool with Herman.[9]

By 10:00 p.m., Murphy ran out of money and wanted to cash a check. Herman watched in awe as Murphy pulled out his long wallet filled with checks that spilled onto the bar. The check on top of the stack was for $15, written by the owner of Neeld's Florist in Tampa, Herman's former landlady. Because Herman knew Mrs. Neeld, he readily cashed the check for Murphy. He knew how conservative Mrs. Neeld was and thought, "Murphy must be an ace salesman to sell her something."[10]

Herman was impressed with Murphy's job. For hours they talked about how Murphy was his own boss and traveled the states east of the Mississippi River for the National Florist Directory. When Herman asked about the possibility that he might travel for NFD, Murphy, under the influence of at least a dozen glasses of beer, said, "Well, I'll just hire you." They pledged to meet at the bar the following morning. Herman told Murphy to be sure and knock at the door if the bar was closed.

Herman was excited. He remembered, "What more is there? Getting to travel and make lots of money, all at the same time!"[11]

Murphy never appeared on Sunday morning. After the salesman did not come to the bar on Monday, Herman called the information operator in Leachville, Arkansas, to get the number for NFD. When he called the company, Leona Short, the wife of NFD owner, Ken Short, answered the phone. Herman asked, "When do I go to work?"[12]

Mrs. Short informed Herman that her husband and Murphy were out of town but she would send Herman an application for employment. Herman completed the application and called Mrs. Short on several occasions during the next week. Finally, Mrs. Short said, "I still haven't talked to Dale or my husband. Don't call again. They'll call you." Herman was persistent. He told Mrs. Short, "I really need to get this job!"

Within a few days, Ken Short called Herman at a pay phone which was the only telephone in the bar. Herman related the story of how Murphy had promised him a job and that he was excited about going to work for NFD. Short and Murphy were at the Hotel Severin in Indianapolis, Indiana, at the time of the call. Short covered the phone, looked across at the other bed where Murphy was sitting, and said, "This guy by the name of Herman Meinders said you hired him at his bar." Murphy had a blank look on his face because he did not remember anything about the night at Sammy's Bar, much less the fact that he had hired Herman as an NFD salesman.[13]

However, Short had found it difficult to hire salesmen who were willing to just "pick up and travel all over the nation," so he asked Herman when he could begin. Herman replied, "I can leave here in 30 minutes." Short could sense the excitement in Herman's voice and invited him to join Murphy in Indianapolis.[14]

In the next few minutes, Herman announced to his partner and customers that he had a job and was leaving for Indiana within the hour. One customer, Dale Beck, said he

Ken Short, right, and his wife, Leona, founded the National Florist Directory with headquarters in Leachville, Arkansas. The Shorts gave Herman his first job in the floral industry.

needed to get to Ohio and promised that if he could ride with Herman that far, he would give him a place to stay, a hot meal, and enough money to buy gas to travel on to Indianapolis.

Herman loaded all his worldly goods into his green 1949 Studebaker he had driven since going to college. The car had a scratched windshield and a hole in the trunk that had been inflicted when someone broke into the car and stole his spare tire and jack.

Childers gave Herman $15 and five watches taken in lieu of cash on bar bills. After saying goodbye to Childers and friends in the bar, Herman and Beck left Tampa in the evening hours of March 8, 1958.

Not long after beginning the trip, Herman was stopped

for speeding in Lake City, Florida. The sheriff who pulled him over asked for his wallet and driver's license. The sheriff confiscated the $15 cash and said, "Now son, don't speed anymore." Herman was broke, but called the bar collect and was promised a Western Union cash transfer within the next few hours.[15]

Herman picked up the cash at a Western Union/ flower shop in southern Georgia and resumed his trip toward Ohio and Indiana. Early in the morning, they arrived in front of a large, white house in the small Ohio town where his passenger lived. When they walked up to the front door, a woman opened it, looked at Beck, and said, "I told you I never wanted to see you again!" She slammed the door in their faces, and Beck said, "Well, I guess she's still mad at me!"[16]

Without apology, Beck told Herman, "Well, kid, you're on your own. I don't know what you're gonna' do." Beck started walking and left Herman and his car in front of the house.

Herman had few options, so he went back to the door and knocked. He told the angry Mrs. Beck, "I know you're mad at him, but I've got to tell you my predicament. I have driven all night with a promise that you would let me take a bath, fix me breakfast, and loan me enough money for gas to get to Indianapolis." Miraculously, the lady took Herman in, cooked him one of the best breakfasts he ever ate, and gave him $4 for gas.[17]

Herman drove all day toward Indianapolis. At 5:00 p.m., he hit rush hour traffic and had a flat tire on the infamous traffic circle in the city's downtown area. A frantic police officer shouted, "Get out of the way, buddy, move it!" Herman would have liked to hurry and change his tire, but his jack had been stolen. The officer glared at Herman when he told him he did not have a jack.

Herman was directed to a Standard gasoline station about a block away to borrow a jack. The second problem was that Herman's spare tire had been stolen also. A third, seemingly insurmountable problem was that Herman had only 20 cents left in his pocket. Unable to borrow a jack without collateral, he raised his sleeve and showed the attendant the five watches he had left the bar with. The attendant picked out the nicest one to secure the return of the jack. Herman brought the flat tire back to the station to be repaired. When he was informed that it would cost 75 cents to repair the tire, Herman told the attendant that he would have a friend bring the money to the station.[18]

Using one of his remaining two dimes, Herman called the Severin Hotel for Murphy. There was no answer. The station attendant said he was closing within a half hour and needed his money by that time. When he said he would just keep the watch for the repair, Herman told him, "That's too much for just fixing a tire. I'll get the money."

Herman used his last dime to call the hotel again and Murphy answered. Herman told him he was running a little short of money and needed an advance to pay 75 cents to the service station. Murphy, who still did not remember ever meeting Herman, went to the station and paid for the tire repair.[19]

"He looked like a carnival worker," is the way Murphy described Herman when he saw him at the gas station. Herman had on a black leather jacket and wore watches on his arm like someone Murphy had seen hawking watches at a carnival. Murphy had already told his boss what a great guy Herman was, but muttered "Oh, no!" when he saw him.[20]

With his tire repaired, Herman followed Murphy back to the hotel. Herman was anxious to begin his job for the National Florist Directory, although he knew absolutely nothing about the flower business. While driving to the hotel, it certainly never occurred to Herman that his would someday be the most recognizable name in the world's floral industry.

On the Road

CHAPTER 5

IN THE NEXT FEW YEARS, HERMAN VISITED
ALMOST EVERY FLOWER SHOP IN AMERICA.
PETE GARCIA

Herman began the following morning as a trainee
under Dale Murphy, traveling the country for the National
Florist Directory. The company was founded by Ken and Leona
Short. Ken had worked for a National Directory of Morticians
for several years, and his wife, Leona, was a florist. They recognized the need for a national list of flower shops to allow a local
florist to serve its clients by knowing whom to send flowers
through in a distant city. During his travels, Ken Short developed
a fondness for Leachville, Arkansas, just a few miles from the
Missouri-Arkansas border, and based his directory operation in
that city in 1954. The following year, Short hired his first sales
representative, Fred Swindle, and the two of them began traveling the country selling the directory.

Short had been in business only three years when

Herman came on board in 1958. The listing of florists became known as the Redbook because of the color of its cover. When florists called each other with orders, it was much easier to say, "I have a Redbook order for you," than to say, "I have a National Florist Directory order for you."[1]

When Short and his staff of salesmen sold advertisements for the NFD directory, the information was sent to Barbara Grimes. Grimes worked for the company as office manager and publications manager for 40 years. She typed the information and readied it for printing. Her husband, Monte, was later involved when a new company, Florafax, was formed.[2]

Being a professional florist in the United States was still a relatively new occupation in the middle of the 20th century. America's floriculture developed into an industry in the 1870s as crop specialization emerged and floral accessories such as bouquet holders, foil, and ribbon were introduced. Before that, retail flower shops were normally small and attached to a nearby greenhouse. Growers sold flowers directly to urban shops or to peddlers who hawked them on street corners.[3]

In the final years of the 19th century, several groups such as the American Association of Nurserymen and the Society of American Florists (SAF) were formed to share information and provide outlets for long distance orders. However, it was not until 1910 that a group of florists met during a recess of the annual SAF convention to form Florists' Transworld Delivery Association (FTD), America's first flowers-by-wire service.[4] There was a definite need to speed the delivery of flowers between cities and the 6,000 florists in the nation. Americans were sending more flowers to loved ones in distant cities.

By 1958, when Herman joined NFD, approximately half of the florists belonged to one of two major wire services that guaranteed payment for floral orders through a clearinghouse. FTD, the largest wire service company, used a Mercury Man in its logo and became the floral industry's leader in marketing.[5] The second flowers-by-wire service was Telegraph Delivery Service (TDS), founded in 1934 by Edwin S. Douglas.[6] FTD and TDS published directories also, but only of their members.

Thus, the NFD was an idea whose time had come.

The flowers-by-wire concept had worked successfully in the country for decades. For example, a customer at a flower shop in Oklahoma City could pay for an arrangement to be delivered by a florist in Little Rock. The Oklahoma City florist took payment from the customer, kept a percentage for himself, and sent the balance to the Little Rock florist.

Herman had only three days on the road with Dale Murphy to learn how to sell copies of the National Florist Directory and advertisements in the publication that was planned for printing each summer. They began calling on flower shops and greenhouses the morning after Herman met Murphy at the hotel. One of the first stops was at a flower shop/greenhouse combination in a small town near Indianapolis. With ease, they sold the owner, who was planting bedding plants in the greenhouse, a $15 directory and a $10 advertisement for the following year's edition.[7]

However, on the walk from the greenhouse to the flower shop, Herman commented that stormy weather was approaching. He said, "I bet if it hailed, it would knock out the glass and really damage all the plants in this greenhouse." The idea of such a calamity shook the flower shop owner so much that he canceled his order for an ad in the directory. Herman learned at that moment to never mention negative possibilities with a potential customer.[8]

Herman learned another valuable lesson in his first few days on the job—never stay around too long after consummating a sale. He was so happy when he got a check from a customer he kept talking with the young man. When the man's father, his partner, returned to the store, he announced they did not want to buy an ad in the directory and took his check back.

Herman received immediate payment for his sales. His portion of a sale was 50 percent. NFD received 40 percent and Murphy received the remaining 10 percent as an override, at least for awhile. Herman kept a tedious record of sales. He often cashed checks in the same town where he made the sale—local bankers had no problem cashing checks written on their customers' accounts. Times were hard, but only once was Herman forced to call the NFD office to have money wired to him.

Selling directories and ads for NFD was a lonely job. Herman was assigned entire states to canvas and was expected to call on every florist. He lived in a different, low-budget motel or motor court every night. Whenever possible, he stayed at a YMCA for 50 cents to $2.00 a night. He also made a practice of visiting high school classmates who had spread out across the country. Among the classmates who provided free room and board for Herman, the traveling salesman, were Denny and Cathy Crook in New York, Howard Wathen in Minnesota, and Jack and Leila Nessen and Stan Zetterlund in Wisconsin. Herman also stayed with Nessen's father in Arizona and Florida.[9]

By visiting friends, Herman not only saved money, but helped the loneliness of living on the road 50 weeks of the year. Looking back, Herman said, "I could not have made it, financially or emotionally, without the support of my friends."

Herman had no trouble reading maps, especially in small towns and rural areas. However, when he first worked in Cleveland, Ohio, he hired a fireman to drive him around to local flower shops and teach him how to read maps of larger cities.

Early in his floral industry career, Herman recognized that it paid dividends to attend floral conventions at which he met many future customers and made lifelong friends. In 1959, at the Arkansas state convention of florists, he met Ann Hobbs, a floral wholesaler in Little Rock, Arkansas. It was Hobbs' first convention. She remembered, "I was impressed with his vast knowledge of the industry, especially when I found out he had only been on the road for a year. His enthusiasm helped me begin to love the industry and its people."[10]

Herman averaged driving 88,000 miles a year from 1958 to 1967. He called on every floral shop in 37 states, many shops in the remaining states, and some provinces in Canada. Herman's travel experiences could fill an entire book. Dale Murphy, the man responsible for Herman having the job, reflected, "No one ever worked harder or made more calls than Herman."[11]

Herman was not a slow driver, and often was stopped

by police for speeding. Some states had a policy of keeping a violator's driver's license pending disposition of the case, so Herman obtained licenses in more than a dozen states. The system worked for him—if he was stopped, and his license taken, he used a license from another state on his next encounter with police. This was long before law enforcement agencies were linked by computer to detect use of multiple licenses.

Pete Garcia, who later established one of the most successful floral hard goods companies in America, was also a traveling salesman in the late 1950s and 1960s when Herman spent most of his time on the road. Garcia, who often crossed paths with Herman, remembered, "We were a special fraternity—road warriors. Herman and I both ran up a bunch of mileage. There were a lot of worn-out tires, calloused hands, and worn-out pants from sitting so long in cars."[12]

The lonely road caused Herman to welcome passengers. Once in West Virginia during the winter, a service station owner asked Herman to give a sailor a ride. The sailor was on his way to Ohio. A few miles out of town, the sailor asked Herman, "Who do you have in the trunk?" Herman said there was no one and that maybe the sailor was hearing ice from the roof of the car falling onto the trunk. When they arrived at a diner, Herman opened the trunk to assure the sailor that no one was there. The diner was closed, so they continued on their trip. The man was hallucinating so badly that Herman let him out of the car at a gas station in the next community. Herman never knew what happened to the sailor.[13]

Herman was kind to potential customers—but tenacious. Ken Benjamin, a pioneer in floral publications, met Herman at conventions and trade shows and heard stories from florists who had succumbed to Herman's sales pitch. Benjamin said, "He was the kind of guy who would go into a shop, put his feet on the table, have a cup of coffee, and stay overnight. He considered florists his friends, and did not leave if he thought there was a possibility of a sale. Many times, florists told me they finally said, 'OK, for God's sake, sign me up!'"[14]

Herman never really liked coffee, but always accepted

a cup from a potential customer just to be friendly. "It always seemed to me that the last cup was worse than the cup before, so I began to suspect that florists called ahead to see how bad the next person could make coffee," he remembered. Herman swore off coffee for good after an experience with a lady florist in Harlingen, Texas.

It was late afternoon and the florist invited Herman to her home to share her birthday cake. Herman obliged but asked for Coke or milk to drink. Unfortunately, all the woman had was coffee. She struck a match, lit a gas stove, and made coffee using a cake pan over an open flame. The coffee was so noxious that Herman thought he surely was being poisoned. He pledged never to drink coffee again—a pledge he has kept for 40 years.[15]

In his first year on the road, Herman once had car trouble in Marshalltown, Iowa. He planned to hitchhike home while a local mechanic repaired the car. However, he did not want to start home in the middle of the night. He had only a $2 bill in his wallet and opted to sleep in his car, saving his money for breakfast before he started the road trip home.

The next morning, he paid for his breakfast at a local restaurant with the $2 bill. The cashier, thinking it was a $20 bill, gave Herman $18 and some change. Before he walked out the door, Herman wrote the restaurant a check for $18 and handed it to the cashier. She said, "But we don't cash checks." Herman explained that had he not been honest, she would not have the $18 at all. The lady agreed, smiling as she stuck Herman's check into the cash drawer.[16]

Herman drove good cars in his travels. After driving his 1949 Studebaker for a few months, he graduated to a 1953 Ford and then to a new 1959 Ford Galaxy 500. After wearing out a 1960 Ford Sunliner convertible, he bought the best car he ever owned, a red 1961 Ford Thunderbird, purchased at 2:00 a.m. one morning at Courtesy Motor Company in Chicago, Illinois.

The car dealership was ahead of its time with a "no dickering" policy. Many of the salesmen were former car dealers and were sharp and professional. The dealer would not even throw in a set of floor mats to close the deal—the best they would do is flip a coin for the price of the mats. Herman won the coin toss and drove off with his new car and new floor mats. Herman drove the car 136,000 miles and needed only one new set of brakes, a repair job at 70,000 miles while Herman was in Winnipeg, Canada.[17]

Herman eventually traded his Thunderbird for a new Cadillac purchased from Dick Mitchell Cadillac in El Reno, Oklahoma. Thereafter, he annually bought a new Cadillac as his sales commissions increased. During his years with NFD, Herman averaged earning $55,000 yearly in commissions, although he had to pay his expenses. Once, when Herman threatened to look for a better paying job, NFD owner Short raised Herman's commission to 60 percent of sales—Dale Murphy lost his 10 percent override.[18]

Herman believed that every time he drove a nicer car, his customers noticed, and it improved sales. He remembered, "If you looked prosperous and confident, the florist you had never met before believed in you and bought a directory."[19]

All records kept by the nine NFD salesmen were kept by hand. Herman's reports were written legibly and were easy to understand. Office manager Barbara Grimes recalled, "He was fun to work with. He was never rude and filled out his reports with great care." However, Grimes said Herman always looked like he was hungry.[20]

In 1961, Ken Short established Florafax, a flowers-by-wire service to compete with FTD and TDS. Short devised a plan where a florist filling an order issued a draft for the discounted amount he was owed. The immediate payment was a selling point over FTD and TDS whose members had to wait until the end of the month to receive payment. However, the novel approach actually cost florists more than the other services, so within six months Florafax adopted FTD's method of paying both florists involved in a wire transaction.[21]

Soon Herman was selling for both NFD and Florafax. Bill Plummer, a florist in Morrilton, Arkansas, longtime executive secretary of the Arkansas State Florist Association, and an early Florafax subscriber, remembered Herman as easy to deal with. He said, "We communicated well. Every time I saw Herman, he was the same man, friendly and glad to see me."[22]

Herman was not a high pressure salesman. Bob and Jean Coleman had recently opened a flower shop in Oklahoma City in a small 18-foot store front. Bob Coleman said, "He did not try to get me to sign up with Florafax with any tricks or high pressure—he just explained the benefits and made it an option for us. If we wanted the service, we could have it—if we couldn't afford the service at the moment, he was still our friend and treated us the same."[23]

Herman also on occasion trained new salesmen for Florafax. Larry Hendershott, the son of the director of the University of Georgia horticulture department, spent three days on the road with Herman, the same training time that Herman was given with Dale Murphy. [24]

Hendershott closely observed how Herman walked into a floral shop for the first time and made friends within minutes, usually making a sale. He also learned just how much time Herman spent on the road. One evening when they were dining, Herman told the waitress he wanted prime rib, but only if it was fresh and not pre-frozen. When the meat came out of the kitchen, Herman took one bite and said, "I'm sorry, but this was not cut from a large piece of prime rib—this was pre-frozen and you just thawed it out." Herman ate at restaurants so much that he could immediately tell the difference in quality.[25]

Also in 1961, Herman decided to sell directories and Florafax subscriptions to florists in Hawaii. He invited his old friend, Jack Nessen, to accompany him to Hawaii to call on florists and to visit Herman's brother, Don, who was on active duty in the United States Army.

Herman and Nessen headed for California in Herman's Thunderbird, but Herman had not informed Nessen that he was going to visit every florist in New Mexico. The trip took a week.[26]

Herman drove the Thunderbird literally 90-miles-an-hour across the Southwest. Nessen remembered, "Sometimes we were airborne. In the desert, drainage was provided by huge dips in the road. When Herman hit them at such great speed, we flew for a few feet before hitting the ground hard."[27]

Herman and Nessen arrived in California expecting to catch a ship bound for Hawaii—they assumed daily voyages left the West coast. However, when they discovered ocean passage was not available for two weeks, they bought discount

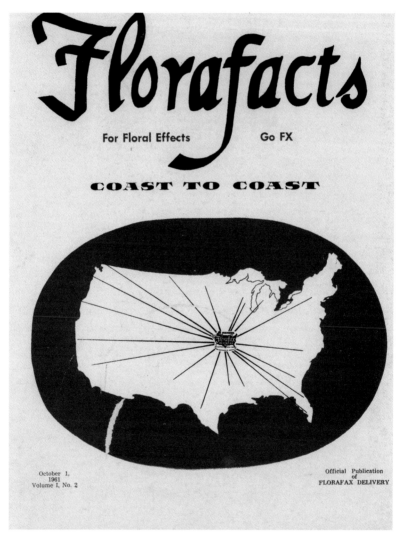

The Florafax directory was published under the title, *Florafacts.* **Florafax was founded by Ken Short in 1961 as a companion company to the National Florist Directory.**

One of Herman's mentors in the floral industry was Harry Killian, general manager of Florafax. Killian was an old-fashioned, strict manager who had overseen floral arrangements at the White House under four presidents. He later worked for Herman at American Floral Services.

tickets on a very cheap non-scheduled charter airline, Transcontinental Airlines.

At the airport, hundreds of people lined up to get one of the 300 seats on the airplane. Herman stood in line while Nessen sat in the lounge, comfortable with the fact that he had a ticket. An hour later, Nessen stepped in front of Herman in the line as they approached the entrance to the ramp to the airplane. After the agent took Nessen's ticket, he looked at Herman and said, "That's it. That's 300 people. We'll be flying again in three days."[28]

Herman was incensed, yelling, "I've got a boarding pass and I'm getting on that plane." The agent said, "There's no room!" Herman would not accept the agent's decision, handed him a $20 bill, grabbed a boarding pass and ran past Nessen, screaming, "Jack, if you wanna' fly with me, you better hurry!" They ran fast and got ahead of other people in the line and found a seat.

The plane flew from Burbank to San Francisco where several passengers were removed because the aircraft was overloaded. Luckily, Herman and Nessen were able to stay onboard for the flight across the Pacific Ocean to Hawaii.[29]

The trip took many hours in the lumbering, propeller-driven aircraft. Once they arrived, Herman and Nessen were tired and wanted to sleep. But the tour guide announced that all purchasers of the Hawaii package were required to report at 7:00 a.m. the next day for a tour of the island.

While visiting Oahu, Herman added to his growing driver's license collection. He obtained an Hawaii license, which at the time was granted for life.

Herman also took scuba diving lessons from one of his brother's friends. However, it turned out the soldier had little experience in teaching scuba diving. Herman donned diving gear and air tanks and, without any instruction, was told, "Well, you just jump off into the water." Herman did and dropped like a lead weight deep into the ocean. To this day, he does not remember how he escaped the weighted suit and returned to the surface.[30]

Founding a Dream

CHAPTER 6

HERMAN WAS FIRM IN HIS CONVICTIONS.
HE WOULD LISTEN TO OTHER PEOPLE, BUT WAS
HARD TO SWAY WHEN HE KNEW HE WAS RIGHT.
HE WAS A GAMBLER.
ELMER SCHIENBEIN

Life on the road selling listings and ads for the National Florist Directory prepared Herman for a bright future in the floral business. In the span of a few years, he made contact with more florists than most would have in a lifetime. With his friendly manner, the florists became not only customers, but lifelong friends.

Herman's friends and customers were spread from coast to coast. In Phoenix, Arizona, Elmer Schienbein, a former mechanical engineer from Canada, owned 10 retail shops. Walter Metz, after completing a tour in the United States Air Force, opened a retail flower shop in South Florida. Other early customers included John Byerly of Denver, Colorado; George Schulze of Pipestone; Alan Preuss of Milwaukee, Wisconsin; Wayne

Babb of Olathe, Kansas; Terry Eidson of Kansas City, Kansas; Sandy White of Memphis, Tennessee; Willie Lee, Lyndon, and Basil Holt of Dallas, Texas; Mildred Riddle of Midland, Texas; Paul Wentland of Chicago, Illinois; and Gula Adams of Las Animas, Colorado.

In the early years of selling for NFD, Herman tried to make it back home to Pipestone to see his family as often as possible. Herman always made it home for Christmas. Younger sister, Linda, said "It was special because there was so much snow and Herman got to stay longer than normal."[1]

When at home, Herman still played pinochle into the night with his family. If Herman was in town over the weekend, the men stayed up late on Saturday night, teasing each other about the quality of the hands they were dealt. No matter how late they played, Herman's mother rousted everyone out of bed on Sunday morning to attend St. Paul Lutheran Church, followed by a world-class German Sunday dinner.

Herman played an important role as the oldest child in the Meinders family. "Our father looked up to him because he knew he was the one to carry on the family traditions," his sister, Linda, remembered. That trust was well-placed because Herman has been able to keep the family together, especially for holidays, decades after the late night pinochle games in the Meinders farmhouse in cold Minnesota. Herman was also thoughtful of his sisters and brothers. Linda will never forget when she received her first pair of ice skates from Herman one Christmas.[2]

Herman had an unorthodox way to make certain he called on every flower shop in a town he was canvassing. He simply pulled alongside a telephone booth and tore out the yellow pages' listings of florists. He kept the listings for the next year, but put the information on 3 x 5 index cards. The country was wide open for sales for NFD, as some salesmen were older or married and did not want to venture beyond the six or seven states around Leachville, Arkansas. Herman lived out of his car, so if Massachusetts needed working, he gassed up his car and headed that way.[3]

He stayed in a different place every night, unless he was working in a large city such as Pittsburgh, Pennsylvania. In

In 1967, Florafax expanded into Mexico. Herman made many friends on sales trips to that country. Left to right, Jose Garcia, president of the Monterrey, Mexico Florists Association; Paul Cole, Florafax vice president of public relations, and two other Mexican florists.

big cities, Herman rented a small apartment for a week. As he made more money, he moved out of the YMCA's into better quality motels and hotels. He always traveled light, but was well-dressed—having accumulated a nice wardrobe while working at J.C. Penney.[4]

After a few years with NFD and Florafax, Herman began working the Western states. Ken Short expanded his national sales force, but no salesman wanted to call on flower shops that were many miles apart in the West. However, Herman just drove faster and shortened his presentation. One of his successful methods was to convince florists to be listed in more than just the city in which they were located. For example, a Pipestone florist might be listed under neighboring towns such as Jasper, Holland, and Troskey, so that a florist wanting to send flowers to those towns would be directed to him.[5]

Herman continued to spend most of his time on the road. As he crisscrossed the country, he spent more and more time in Oklahoma City, dating Judith "Judy" Flaherty of El Reno, Oklahoma. Her parents were Ray and Ruth Flaherty. Ray worked for Rock Island Railroad and had part-time jobs at the

Youngheims's local clothing store and El Reno Monument Company.[6]

Herman and Judy were married on August 17, 1963, and began looking for a permanent home, an idea that was foreign to Herman because he had spent most of the previous five years living out of a suitcase. They found a duplex and a garage apartment on North Classen Boulevard in Oklahoma City that could be purchased for $21,500.

Herman, right, as vice president of sales for Florafax, represented the company in 1968 in presenting an eight-foot floral blanket to the winner of the world's richest horse race, the All American Quarter Horse Futurity, at Ruidoso, New Mexico.

In November, Herman's application to buy the property was approved by Mutual Federal Savings and Loan. The closing was set for the afternoon of November 22. When the world learned shortly after lunch of the assassination of President John F. Kennedy in Dallas, Herman's father-in-law tried to talk him out of buying the property, feeling that the country would surely go into recession. However, Herman and Judy decided to go through with the purchase and became the proud owners of the property at 4610 North Classen Boulevard.[7]

For awhile, Judy traveled with Herman. But wanting to establish a home, she moved into the second story of the duplex—she felt safer there with Herman gone most of the time. They rented out the first story of the duplex and the garage apartment located on the back of the lot to lessen the impact of the monthly payment on their loan.

In the spring of 1966, Judy was pregnant so Herman tried to plan his road trips to make certain he would be in Oklahoma City on April 15, the projected date of birth. However, Kathryn Ann "Kathy" Meinders came early, born on March 31 at Mercy Hospital in Oklahoma City. Herman was in south Texas when he received the call that Judy was in labor.

Herman immediately headed toward Oklahoma City. He was stopped for speeding in Austin, Texas, and had to cash a check at Connelly-Hillen Florist to pay the fine. Ironically, Bernie Hillen was the president of FTD. Kathy was a few hours old when Herman arrived in Oklahoma City.[8]

When Kathy was two months old, she and her mother began traveling with Herman as he called on florists in his territory. She grew up attending conventions and flower shows, and made hundreds of new friends at floral shops around the nation.[9]

In 1967, Florafax built a new building in Leachville, Arkansas, and expanded its operations to accommodate the growth of the Redbook and Florafax. Being on the road most of the year, Herman missed his family, so he took a large cut in pay to move to Leachville to become Florafax's sales manager. He later was named vice president of sales.[10]

Herman bought the nicest house in Leachville. It was filled with beautiful mahogany woodwork and was located on an acreage with a creek in the back. Judy worked in the Florafax office part-time.

Being in the Florafax headquarters taught Herman another side of the flowers-by-wire business—things to do and things not to do. Florafax had grown to 3,000 members, but had signed up 6,000 florists to get there. Herman recognized the Florafax method of charging the $30 annual membership in one payment was a hindrance to florists renewing. Herman knew if he owned the business, he would charge the same annual membership, but bill it in increments on the monthly statement.[11]

During the thousands of hours driving America's back roads and highways, Herman was thinking—planning on the day when he might have an opportunity to own his own business. The opportunity came much sooner than expected.

In March, 1970, Ken Short sold Florafax. Rex Rudy represented the buyer and spent a lot of time with Short. That summer, Rudy took Herman aside and hinted strongly that the new owners might be making personnel changes. Rudy told Herman, "Some of the new executives will be moving here to join the company and will be looking for homes. You have the nicest house in town—so you ought to consider selling."[12]

Herman took Rudy's advice, sold the house, and was always grateful to Rudy for his prediction of what lay ahead at the company. But Herman remained at Florafax for the time being.

Herman remembered the very moment—1:30 p.m. on October 22, 1970, when he learned from a florist friend that the latest edition of the Florafax directory showed Herman had been demoted from vice president of sales to a sales representative for Minnesota, Wisconsin, and North and South Dakota.

Herman said, "I was incensed that my florists knew of my demotion before I did."[13] It took Herman only two minutes to decide that Florafax was not in his future. At 1:32 p.m., he resigned and gave his two weeks notice. He decided to return to Oklahoma City to build his own business.

One night, while sitting in a bar across the street from the Brown Palace Hotel in Denver, Colorado, after attending a florists convention, Herman shared his ideas and the search for a name for his company with Mackey Hord, who worked for Denver Wholesale Florist. Herman told Hord that he wanted a name that began with the letter "a" so that his business would always appear near the front of any listing in telephone books and yellow pages.[14]

A week later, Hord called with his 13-year-old son's suggestion that Herman's new business be called something that began with the word, "American." Herman liked the idea.

Right: Herman, right, and the first AFS employee, LuCille Tudor, check contracts received from sales representatives. Their desks were placed together because both officed in a tiny room in the garage apartment where AFS began.

Left: Herman's daughter, Kathy, at her "desk" in a closet of the AFS headquarters on North Classen Boulevard in Oklahoma City.

American Floral Services, Inc., (AFS) was incorporated, and began business in Herman's 900-square-foot garage apartment in November, 1970. It was a bare beginning. Herman started the company with only $500—but he had incredible determination and knew the flowers-by-wire business better than anyone in the nation. He had attended 42 floral conventions one year while working for Florafax, and personally knew many of the florists in the United States.[15]

Herman needed a secretary, and looked in *The Daily Oklahoman* at advertisements listing workers looking for jobs. On a Saturday night about 7:30 p.m., he called the number listed in an ad purchased by LuCille Tudor, who had just moved to Oklahoma City. LuCille, who had received several crank and obscene calls because of the ad, almost hung up on Herman

The first AFS logo was introduced in early 1971. Sales representatives used window stickers of the logo to get the name of the new company out to the nation's florists.

because he began the conversation, "Come on over to the apartment now for an interview!" LuCille heard a baby crying in the background as Herman said, "Judy, keep the baby quiet, I'm trying to take care of business."[16]

Even though she was leery of the opportunity, LuCille needed a job and told Herman that she and her husband would appear for an interview the following morning. Herman invited the Tudors into the apartment for coffee and hired AFS's first employee on the spot, without checking references or asking much about her skills.

With his office staff—LuCille—in place, Herman began looking for sales representatives who would work on a

C.E. "Duke" Rohrbacher, left, and Tommye Williams, were the first two sales representatives hired by Herman to call on florists and convince them to join AFS.

commission basis. Within a few days, sales representatives were on the road, calling on Herman's old friends and potential customers. Herman brought Harry Bernard, Tommye Williams,

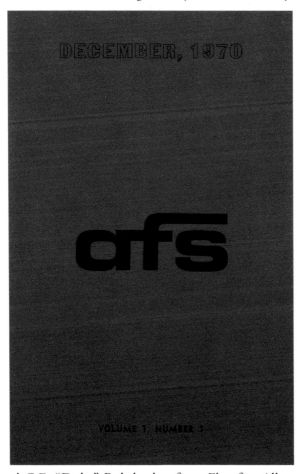

The first American Floral Services directory was published in December, 1970. The reddish-orange Day-Glo color was intentionally used to make the book easy for florists to identify. The first AFS directory, 6" by 9," was19 pages with 137 florists listed. The FTD directory for that month was more than 400 pages with 13,000 listings. The Florafax directory was even larger, 457 pages. When AFS was sold in 1994, three different directories were published with a total of more than 5,000 pages.

and C.E. "Duke" Rohrbacher from Florafax. All were veteran salespeople. Malcolm W. "Mac" McClellan, who was new to the industry, also came on board and became a top notch salesman as well as vice president of corporate development. In addition, Herman was constantly on the telephone with florists with whom he had become good friends.[17]

The fledgling idea worked. Because of Herman's stellar reputation of honesty and integrity, florists began changing their allegiance from Florafax, TDS, and FTD and became members of the AFS system.

The garage apartment on North Classen Boulevard in Oklahoma City where American Floral Services had its beginning in 1970.

American Floral Services, Inc. was incorporated with Herman as president, Judy as Treasurer, Mac McClellan as vice president, and Carl Bagwell as secretary. Bagwell was an Oklahoma City attorney who prepared the incorporation papers and represented AFS for many years.

There were still difficult times ahead. Cash flow was a problem in the early years of AFS. Many times, Herman would wait for the morning mail to receive checks to deposit so he could pay his employees. One December morning in 1970, Herman was second-guessing himself for starting AFS. He had little money and most florists he called still expressed their opinions that America did not need another floral wire service. However, Herman was encouraged by a letter he received that day from John Walker, executive vice president of the Society of American Florists (SAF). Walker told Herman, "You can do it! You know so many people in the industry and they all trust you!"[18]

LuCille did everything—kept books and records and coordinated the travels of sales representatives. She also began a monthly in-house newsletter, "Scribblings," in which she reported on the growth of the company and included short biographical sketches of employees.

The front room of the garage apartment was a telephone center that contained three telephones and a portable typewriter on a used desk. Herman and LuCille occupied two

Above: The second home of American Floral Services was 1,300 square feet of rented office space in an insurance company building across the street from the garage apartment where AFS was founded. *Left:* A cake helped celebrate the first anniversary of AFS in 1971. Left to right, Malcolm W. "Mac" McClellan, AFS vice president for corporate development; Judy Meinders; Herman; and AFS attorney Carl Bagwell.

Herman and his first two office employees at AFS, LuCille Tudor, right, and Paula Bussing. Herman hired LuCille as the first AFS staff member by answering an advertisement in *The Daily Oklahoman*.

desks set side by side in the other room.[19]

AFS's first floral directory contained a listing of only 137 florists, serving 307 cities in the United States. In comparison with other floral directories, the AFS book was small, but its reddish-orange Day-Glo cover made it stand out from other directories.

The tiny staff sometimes worked all night calling out orders. As a service to its subscribers, AFS even took orders for cities and towns that were not listed in the AFS directory. It was a bonus when an order actually was going to another of the handful of AFS subscribers.[20]

Herman was determined that AFS would not be like other wire services. He shocked the industry by introducing the practice of no-charge sending of floral orders. The sending florist was not charged a clearinghouse fee that was levied against florists sending orders by FTD, Teleflora, and Florafax. The no-charge method was unheard of, but later became an industry standard.[21]

Officials of FTD, the industry leader, publicly stated their company would never stoop to such actions. However, just five years later, in October, 1975, FTD followed AFS's lead by announcing that florists would not be charged a fee for sending an order.[22]

In January, 1971, Duke Rohrbacher became the AFS vice president of sales. Rohrbacher was a tremendous help to Herman in building and training a national sales force. Paula Bussing was also added to the staff to help LuCille with the company's growing volume of paperwork.

When Herman received a copy of the FTD directory in October, 1975, that announced FTD would adopt AFS's policy of not charging florists a fee for originating orders, he wrote on the cover of the directory, "Always keep this copy."

OCTOBER/NOVEMBER 1975

FTD NEWS
MEMBERSHIP LIST

IT'S HERE
NO-CHARGE SENDING
PLUS REDUCED
CLEARING CHARGES

On all FTD orders received for processing
on and after October 1, 1975

Your FTD Board of Directors voted September 12 to eliminate all charges paid by sending florists on FTD orders. The Board also voted to reduce total advances paid on FTD orders from six percent to five percent.

This means that florists sending FTD orders the FTD way will not be charged any advances effective October 1, 1975, and that filling florists will be charged only five percent on the gross amount of each order.

SEND YOUR ORDERS THE FTD WAY!

Within six months, AFS had outgrown the tiny garage apartment. Herman found 1,300 square feet of rental space across the street in a two-story office building at 4509 North Classen Boulevard. The first corporate move in June, 1971, was simple. Herman borrowed a two-wheel dolly to move a few pieces of office furniture and boxes of records to the new location.

A big bonus of the new location was that Herman for the first time had his own office. When a national floral society official called to say he would be visiting AFS, LuCille went to a local library and checked out pictures to hang on the AFS office walls. After the official left, LuCille returned the wall adornments to the library.[23]

By December, 1971, AFS passed the 1,000-member mark with 1,205 florists. Harry Tokunaga was Area Director for 23 sales representatives that fanned out from Oklahoma City to call on the florists of America.

American Floral Services was off and running.

Steady Growth

CHAPTER 7

FLORISTS KNEW HERMAN SO WELL THEY WOULD
JOIN AFS BASED UPON HIS REPUTATION ALONE.
ROBERT H. MEINDERS

Herman's familiarity with florists brought custom-ers to AFS. Dean White, who began his business with one floral shop in Wichita, Kansas, trusted Herman, and immediately began using AFS. From the beginning, White thought Herman would succeed with AFS because he had great public relations skills like NFD and Florafax owner Ken Short, and even better business skills.[1]

"He understood the free spirit of florists," remembered Dallas florist Jane Levieux, "and identified with us, our families, and our problems." The more than half million miles Herman had spent on the road for NFD, getting to know the nation's retail and wholesale florists, paid handsome dividends.[2]

Herman built a loyal team of AFS employees because he was honest with them. In the first few years, no one made a lot of money, but Herman convinced his workers that the idea of AFS was sound and that teamwork would bring positive results.

LuCille Tudor and Ann Truscott worked miracles in the office to make certain that checks arrived in the mail in sufficient numbers to cover expense checks that had been written. Herman said, "They were concerned about me. They also had much faith in me, a fact that kept me going and drove me to work 18 hours a day to assure the company's success."[3] The small band of workers became a family.

Herman had an agreement with Guaranty Bank & Trust that AFS overdrafts up to $5,000 would automatically be covered—however, his employees were not aware of the arrangement. In July, 1971, when Herman was out of town at a convention in Minneapolis, Minnesota, LuCille opened the mail and discovered an overdraft notice of nearly $5,000.

Unable to reach Herman, she and Ann went to their

The first American Floral Services sales meeting was held in Oklahoma City in 1972. Left to right, Harry Tokunaga, Willie Lee Baumgardner, E.J. Batt, Carl Baumgardner, Herman, and Mac McClellan. In the early days of the company, Herman could not pay huge salaries so he offered Duke Rohrbacher and McClellan two percent of the ownership of the company in lieu of higher salaries. Rohrbacher chose a higher salary, but McClellan chose to own part of the company. Herman later bought McClellan's shares, long before AFS became a multi-million dollar company.

Early AFS sales representative Harry Tokunaga, second from left, talks with Judy Meinders' parents, Ruth and Ray Flaherty, at an AFS sales banquet.

own banks during the lunch hour and pooled what little savings they had to cover the overdraft. When Herman returned from the convention two days later, he was informed of their actions, and immediately reimbursed them.[4]

More than 20 years later, Herman had dinner with LuCille and Ann. He told them that he had never paid them interest on the money they had withdrawn from their personal savings accounts. To their shock, he handed them each $1,000 in cash, and again thanked them for the favor they had done for him.[5]

Herman believed so much in the future success of AFS he convinced his younger brother, Robert "Bob" Meinders, an accountant, to join the company in January, 1972. Bob left a successful job at an accounting firm in Pipestone to become the AFS director of finance. From the day Bob arrived on the job, Herman had a sense of relief that he no longer had to worry about the accounting system and money flow—he completely trusted Bob.

A passion for customer service permeated the thinking of all employees at AFS. Under Herman's leadership, everyone was sales-oriented. Herman remembered, "I was aware of companies that had failed because their initial enthusiasm for sales had grown cold, and their emphasis was on creating new products. At AFS, it was everybody's job to sell."[6]

One of the first salespeople for AFS was Basil Holt, whose parents were both florists. Holt joined AFS in early 1972. He had known Herman from working in his parents' floral shop in Dallas. He remembered the lean times during his first assignment at AFS, "We didn't fly to appointments—we drove."

Holt's first calls were in Arizona and California. His attitude was, "I better sell something or I'm dead in the water." Holt actually lost about $1,200 his first year on the road for AFS but believed in Herman's idea and stuck with it, a very wise decision.[7]

Holt introduced himself to florists by walking in the door and saying, "I'm with AFS, flowers by wire." Often, a humorous florist might say, "What is AFS? Is that a disease or something?" Holt would laugh but tell the customer, "Right now, we need you and you need us." His sincerity was evident and customers listened.[8]

Holt found leads where he could. Once, a florist in Torrance, California, took him to the Los Angeles flower market and introduced him to several growers who wholesaled flowers to retail shops. The flower market started early in the morning, with many growers making daily deals between 2:00 and 5:00 a.m. The early hours did not bother Holt, who hung out at a Japanese coffee shop in the market and met many florists who later became customers.[9]

Once a subscriber signed with AFS, Herman wanted to keep them as part of the system forever. Darrell Lake, an early AFS sales representative, said, "Herman wanted every single shop to stay in the directory."[10] If a shop canceled, Herman sent a sales representative for a personal visit with the florist. If that did not work, regional representatives such as Lake called the florist. Lake remembered, "We tried very hard, because a final cancellation had to go through Herman, and that was not news we liked to deliver to him."[11]

As Herman oversaw the sales effort of the company, Bob Meinders took over the accounting and banking responsibilities of the growing company. "Bob was important to our success because I trusted him to completely take care of the business side," Herman remembered. It was a perfect match for AFS—Herman, the master salesman, and Bob, the impeccable accountant.

Because sales were so critical, Herman sacrificed to make certain his salespeople were paid quickly and adequately. He would refrain from taking his own check some weeks so he could reimburse salesmen for expenses the day the expense report arrived at the AFS office.[12]

Carl and Willie Lee Baumgardner were critical to the early success of AFS—both were indispensable sales representatives.

Herman's management style endeared him to his employees. He was not "too good" to perform any task in the company. He often opened the mail and took deposits to the bank. Whatever needed doing, Herman did it. He became involved in employees' lives. He went to see them in the hospital if they were sick and never failed to congratulate employees on births of children and express sadness at their losses of loved ones.[13]

Because of the smallness of the company, everyone was involved in the creation and mailing of a monthly directory. AFS had no mailing service, so everyone pitched in to form an assembly line. One person placed the directory in a plastic bag—others sealed the bags with an electric sealer and added address labels. Cross-training was a necessity, not just a luxury. Because of the exposure to different tasks, employees often asked Herman to transfer into a different job because they liked the new tasks.[14]

Herman not only impressed his employees with his passion for hard work, he also made a huge impression on a young accountant, Bill Winkler, who worked for Foster Dickinson, a CPA firm that performed annual audits of AFS. Winkler, later

Above: **Herman points to his AFS Oklahoma license plate on his Cadillac in front of the new AFS offices in Oklahoma City in 1974.** *Right:* **In February, 1974, American Floral Services moved into its first company-owned building at 3401 Northwest 50th Street in Oklahoma City.**

the chief operating officer of the state's largest advertising agency, Ackerman McQueen, said, "Herman was my hero. I heard stories of the humble beginning of his business and thought to myself, 'Here is a guy who willed his success.'"[15]

Sixteen people attended the AFS national sales meeting held in Oklahoma City in December, 1972. Officers and marketing counselors who attended were Carl Baumgardner, Tommye Williams, Willie Lee Baumgardner, LuCille Tudor, Herman and Judy Meinders, Leonard Drake, Richard Tokunaga, Chris Christiansen, Paul Marvin, Mike Shulack, Harry Tokunaga, Bob Granger, Joseph Fumes, Basil Holt, and Harry Bernard.

Subscriptions in 1972 jumped to 1,763 with an average order of $11.04. Sandra Patnaude joined the company in February, 1973, spending most of her time calling out orders. Harry Killian became AFS's director of administration in March, 1973.[16]

AFS's third full year of business, 1973, reflected continued growth. There were 3,930 subscribing shops with an average order value of $11.59. Nineteen people attended the 1973 sales meeting at about the time Jan Rundle became credit manager.[17]

The quick growth of the company frankly put AFS into a financial bind. In 1973, Herman and Bob desperately searched for a bank that would make a $75,000 loan to secure the future of the company. Many bankers, as well as the Small Business Administration, turned them down. However, Ed Miller and Malcolm "Mac" Rose at Founders Bank in Oklahoma City liked the Meinders boys and approved the loan, although Rose later admitted that he never quite understood what AFS was all about.[18] Herman pledged all his personal and company assets to secure the loan, which was paid back over a three-year period.

With new capital available, Herman and Bob expanded their operations in 1974. AFS moved into its first company-owned building, a 3,300-square-foot office complex at Northwest 50th Street and Grand Boulevard in Oklahoma City. Donna Corjay joined the AFS sales department just prior to the move to the new building.

In June, 1974, AFS did not have sufficient cash flow to print a monthly directory, so Herman sent florists a directory for June and July. A year later, the company, still short of funds, printed a three-month directory. Frankly, florists liked the idea

The December, 1975-January, 1976 AFS directory.

of not having to re-mark favorite florists each month. Later, AFS began publishing only a quarterly directory.

Also in 1974, AFS introduced Info-Com, a teletype communications system that permitted shop-to-shop electronic transmission of wire orders at a lower cost than by the old telephone method. Herman was ahead of his time—florists appreciated the cost savings, and this enticed them to send their orders to other AFS florists.

By December, 1974, AFS had 4,653 florists on board, very close to the magic number of 5,000 that Ken Short had once told Herman a wire service company would need to be success-ful.[19]

Herman's idea was to treat his customers like kings and queens. Basil Holt remembered, "If we had a problem with a florist and had to go back and pay them some money, we did it, even if it was the florist's fault. It was better to eat a small loss than to suffer a bad reputation."[20]

Herman's reputation and integrity were well known in the floral industry. Holt said, "Many times when a florist was wavering on whether or not to join us, he might look at me and say, 'Well, I don't know, but since it's Herman, I know it surely is a good deal.'"[21] Holt said, "A handshake with Herman was as good as the finest legal document drawn up by the best lawyers in town. His word was as good as gold. He never lied to me or even blew the facts out of proportion."[22]

An example of a florist who respected Herman's integrity was Walter Metz, a leading florist in Florida. Metz had been an early skeptic of AFS. He remembered, "At first, I did not think we needed another wire service, but thought if anyone deserved success in this arena, it was Herman."[23] Metz said, "I joined AFS because of Herman and the attitude of the company. They were accessible, friendly, professional, and oriented toward my success."[24]

In fact, the "S" in AFS stood for service, a quality that florists talked about at meetings and conventions. Metz was a longtime member of FTD but believed the king of the industry had become stuffy and removed from its customers. He said, "You had to go with your head bowed in front of them."[25]

Herman, left, and brother, Bob, in front of the new AFS offices on North-west 50ᵗʰ Street in Oklahoma City in 1974. Bob was an indispensable part of the AFS team. Herman completely trusted Bob to handle the financial affairs of the growing company.

VOLUME 5, NUMBER 3

afs 704 "VALENTINE'S LOVE"

In 1974, because of cash flow problems, Herman stopped publishing a monthly directory. Frankly, florists, who made notations in their directories and earmarked favorite florists in distant cities, liked the idea of having to re-mark their directories every two or three months, rather than monthly. This was the cover of the February-March, 1975 directory.

Herman never intended that AFS be the largest wire service—just the best. He was interested in building his list of subscribers with only quality floral shops. The concept of growth worked. To ensure the company's success, the AFS directory began accepting advertisements in 1975.

In 1980, in an effort to compete more effectively with its main competitor and industry leader, FTD, AFS introduced a rebate of 50 cents per order. When Herman was faced with a comment such as, "That's not very much money," he would pull two quarters from his pocket, throw them into the trash can, and say to the florist, "This is how much you throw away every time you place an order with another wire service."[26]

In retrospect, the order rebate became a successful selling tool for AFS, and later became an industry standard. The rebate and no-charge sending were marketing "hooks" that set AFS aside from its competitors.

AFS introduced "Plus Services," a toll-free 800 number in February, 1976. In August of that year, AFS went international, expanding its services into Mexico.

In November, 1976, the company bought a 12,000-square-foot office building at 3716 Northwest 36th Street in Oklahoma City. To generate income, the first floor of the building was leased to other businesses.

Also in 1976, AFS expanded coverage into Canada. The company had only a few subscribers in Canada until Robert "Bob" Newton, a Toronto, Canada, florist and wire service veteran, contacted Herman. Newton wanted to either start his own wire service in Canada or join forces with one of the companies in the United States. They met and shook hands on a deal. Herman never charged Newton anything for establishing the new venture in Canada. Newton remembered, "When I asked about money, Herman said, 'Let's not talk about money, let's talk about how many customers you can bring for the benefit of both of us.'"[27]

Newton, who became president and a shareholder of AFS-Canada, a subsidiary of American Floral Services, chose to do business with AFS because of Herman's accessibility. Newton first visited a Florafax office, but was forced to wait 90 minutes before an official could see him. However, when he traveled to Oklahoma City, he was given an immediate audience with Herman, who was sitting at his desk completing an expense report.[28]

At AFS headquarters in 1976, there were 24 office

workers and 20 sales representatives calling on florists across the North American continent. By the end of that year, AFS had 5,445 subscribers with an average order of $14.13.

Bob and Eulalah Overmeyer joined AFS in February, 1977. Bob was vice president of sales and Eulalah was director of industry relations. Harry Bernard was vice president of major accounts, Harry Killian was vice president of administration, and Basil Holt was named to head the company's new international division.

In December, 1977, Eulalah Overmeyer was promoted to vice president of industry relations, the first woman to hold such a lofty position in the worldwide floral industry. With more than 25 years of experience and as past president of the American Institute of Floral Designers (AIFD), Eulalah earned the distinctive title of "First Lady of the Floral Industry."

Herman continued to spend many hours each day running his business. His marriage to Judy ended in divorce, and

Left to right, Herman's stepdaughter, Suzanne Sloan; daughters, Christy and Kathy; and stepson, Frederick Sloan, in 1978.

Herman later married Jodi Boren. Their daughter, Christine Marie "Christy" Meinders was born September 18, 1977, in Oklahoma City. Christy was named for Christine Boren, the mother of then Oklahoma Governor, and later United States Senator and University of Oklahoma President, David L. Boren.

Herman with his daughters, Kathy, standing, and Christy.

Good Times
and Dark Hours

CHAPTER 8

OUR BUSINESS WAS BOOMING
...THEN CAME THE LOWEST POINT OF MY LIFE.
HERMAN MEINDERS

As the number of AFS subscribers increased, Herman and Bob Meinders thought of new ways to keep their customers happy. In addition to providing rebates, they also presented gifts to florists who exceeded certain levels of orders. Herman once bought a truckload of ice cream freezers left over from a less than successful new account promotion by a local savings and loan. He paid $2 for hand-crank and $3 for electric freezers given to AFS subscribers as promotional incentives.[1]

    "Herman possessed a sharp photographic memory," Donna Corjay remembered, "He was extremely quick at grasping new ideas, and just as quick at implementing them. The words 'no' and 'can't' were foreign to him."[2]

AFS hosted its first international convention aboard the USS *Princess*. Left to right, John Lancaster, Herman, Bob Overmeyer, Donna Corjay, and Eulalah Overmeyer. *Courtesy Donna Corjay.*

One of the elements of Herman's success was his accessibility to customers. Johnny Childers, a veteran floral consultant with the Pete Garcia Company of Atlanta, Georgia, saw AFS growing and observed how Herman had a special relationship with his customers. Childers said, "Other wire services operated in an ivory tower, but Herman knew his customers by name and often knew their spouses and children."[3]

"In our business," Childers reflected, "it was hard to find someone who could talk to everyone, from the biggest florist to the newest worker at a convention. Herman had the knack and he always had something nice to say about everybody."[4]

AFS held its first international convention in April, 1978, aboard the USS *Princess*, a Cunard Line cruise ship. The convention ship sailed from Fort Lauderdale, Florida, to San Juan, Puerto Rico, St. Thomas, Virgin Islands, and Nassau in the Bahamas. By the end of 1978, there were 6,492 AFS subscribers.

The following year, the international convention was

aboard Cunard's USS *Countess* with stops in Puerto Rico, Venezuela, the West Indies, and the Virgin Islands. Also, in 1979, AFS extended its international coverage to Puerto Rico and the Virgin Islands and introduced "Flower Fare," the first AFS selection guide.

Terry Torgler was named general manager of AFS in June, 1979. Other staff additions included Robert Self as director of marketing. The company was booming and was recognized as an established competitor to FTD, the industry leader. At that time, Herman's personal problems began to overshadow the success of his company. He spent much of his time worrying about his pending divorce with his wife, Jodi, and the effect it would have on two-year-old Christy.

At 10:00 p.m. one night in the fall of 1979, two Oklahoma City police officers appeared at the door of Herman's apartment and asked him where he had been all evening. The officers obviously had been looking for Herman and thought he was away from the apartment because he had loaned his personal car to an AFS salesman.[5]

Herman was informed he was being arrested on a complaint he had molested Christy. He was devastated. He would never hurt his baby daughter—he loved her too much.

Still in his pajamas, Herman asked to be left alone to change into a shirt and pants so he could accompany the officers to the police station. He was humiliated when the female officer refused to leave the room while he dressed. The officers loaded Herman into the back seat of a squad car and headed toward the Will Rogers station of the Oklahoma City Police Department. At the corner of Northwest 39th Street and Meridian Avenue, the officers pulled into a gas station and met officers in two other police cars. Those officers asked to be listed on the report as assisting in Herman's arrest.[6]

From the Will Rogers station, Herman was taken by police car to the county jail in downtown Oklahoma City. As he was being booked into custody, Herman felt the damning stares of his handlers. He was searched and then beaten by a jailer as he was thrown into a cell with vagrants and drunks. He observed another inmate being beaten by jailers. Herman remembers, "At that moment, I became bitter. I realized that the American concept that I learned as a kid, that an accused person is presumed innocent until proven guilty, was not really true."[7]

The following morning, Herman called his attorney, Carl Bagwell, who brought in criminal defense attorney, Doyle Scott, to help prove Herman's innocence. Herman explained that the accusation surely was connected to the nasty divorce he was going through. He quickly submitted to, and passed, a polygraph test. However, he was still required to surrender a pubic-hair sample for police to use in trying to match Herman to other sex crimes in Oklahoma City.[8]

Nearly 18 hours after the humiliating experience had begun, Herman was released. His brother, Bob, his sister, Linda, his mother, and AFS colleagues Eulalah Overmeyer and Donna Corjay came to Herman's rescue. They convinced him that good would prevail and that he would be eventually cleared of all charges. With the help of his friends and family, Herman was able to return to AFS and face his employees.[9]

In addition to his supporters, Herman was helped by passages in the Lutheran devotional he had been reading just minutes before the police officers arrested him at his apartment. The chapter in *Portals of Prayer,* published by the Missouri Synod of the Lutheran Church, spoke of those who are falsely accused and how they should react to such accusations.

After an emotional time, the justice system found Herman innocent. Doctors swore that Christy had been molested. But because other parties involved would not submit to polygraph examination, Herman never knew if molestation actually occurred or, if it did, who was guilty.[10]

Herman had only one reason to publicly talk about this horrible episode of his life. He said, "I want others to know that it is possible to overcome trying times with faith in God and the support of friends and family."[11]

With his divorce final, Herman was able to turn his full attention to AFS. The 1980 AFS international convention was held aboard the *Queen Elizabeth II* on its voyage in April from New York City to London.

Also in 1980, AFS increased its order rebate program. Florists received a 50 cent rebate on the first nine orders in a month; a 60 cent rebate on orders from 10 to 99; and a rebate of 75 cents per order if a florist had more than 100 orders posted on its monthly statement.

In brochures sent to florists around the nation, benefits of belonging to AFS were compared to other services. For example, the initial amount required to join AFS was $249, compared to $400 at Florafax, $415 at Teleflora, and $550 at FTD. AFS also had the lowest annual fees, and was the only

During his crisis in 1979, Herman, left, depended heavily upon the counsel of Pastor Lester Hall of Immanuel Lutheran Church in Oklahoma City. Pastor Hall and his wife, Irma, accompanied Herman aboard a cruise on the Mississippi Queen.

WIRE SERVICE	OFFERS A $1.00 REBATE TO THE SENDING FLORIST	DOES NOT PENALIZE THE RECEIVING FLORIST
afs	✓	✓
FTD	DOES NOT OFFER A REBATE	✓
Teleflora	DOES NOT OFFER A REBATE	✓
Florafax	✓	TAKES $1.20 AWAY FROM THE RECEIVING FLORIST

THE CHOICE IS SIMPLE ... SEND AFS!

afs   call toll free: 800-654-6707   In Oklahoma & Canada call collect: 405-947-3373

AM 11821

American Floral Services, Inc.
P.O. Box 12309
Oklahoma City, Oklahoma 73157

Return Postage Guaranteed

Left: American Floral Services used mailers to florists to compare its services and costs with the other wire services. Rice Advertising Agency designed many of the early materials. *Below:* In advertising brochures sent to prospective customers, AFS used testimonials from satisfied florists already using the company.

❝ Find me an employee who works 24 hours a day, 7 days a week, with no coffee breaks or vacations, and transmits all wire orders, and I'll show you my AFS-COM! ❞   July 9, 1977   Arthur T. Ito, President, Flower View Gardens, Inc. Los Angeles, California

company to provide rebates.

Much of Herman's time was spent in producing directories, the lifeblood of his company. If there were no directories, there were no orders. In 1979, Steve Cassady became Herman's printer. Cassady, who worked at Times Journal Publishing, remembered, "When he called, he usually needed a directory printed in a very short time. He knew what he wanted—he had a plan and was very organized."[12]

"Herman did not like the word, 'no,'" Cassady said.

"If he wanted something done, he wanted it done today and my job was to figure out how to get it done. I kept him happy—because I somehow figured out how to quickly respond to his request."[13]

In December, 1980, a surprise party celebrated the 10th anniversary of AFS. Oklahoma Governor George Nigh officially declared December 5 as American Floral Services, Inc. Day in Oklahoma. By the end of 1980, AFS had 9,219 florists with an average order value of $18.87.

Floriculture Directions, a Herb Mitchell Associates publication, was offered to AFS members beginning in 1981. It was a monthly newsletter on floral management

You Know What Makes Us Happy?

Above: The American Floral Services advertising department used photographs of Herman and other AFS officials to grace the cover of a pamphlet to tell florists that they would be happy if the florists began sending orders through AFS. *Left:* AFS used bright colors for directories. Herman's idea was that a brightly-colored directory could be more easily located by busy florists when they needed to send flowers via a wire service. This cover pictured the AFS headquarters at 3716 Northwest 36th Street in Oklahoma City.

afs

AMERICAN FLORAL SERVICES, INC.

June - July 1977   Volume 7, Number 7 - 8

Left: Oklahoma Governor George Nigh, seated, signs the proclamation declaring December 5, 1980, as AFS Day in Oklahoma, celebrating the 10th anniversary of the company. Standing, left to right, Bob Meinders, Herman, and attorney Carl Bagwell. *Below:* Herman poses in front of the *Queen Elizabeth II,* the cruise ship on which the 1980 American Floral Services international convention was held.

that could be obtained by AFS subscribers at a discount rate. Herman and his management team looked for other ways to use education of florists to grow AFS and improve the American floral industry.[14]

In February, 1981, AFS began publishing *Faces and Places,* a monthly publication that was printed separately from the AFS directory. *Faces and Places,* edited by Donna Corjay and printed under the supervision of public relations director Bill Carmichael and industry relations vice president Eulalah Overmeyer, featured stories about AFS and its employees and trends in the national floral business. The first issue reported on AFS's first profit seminar in Los Angeles, California. For the seminar, Herman brought in speakers such as Doug Dillon, president of the Society of American Florists, Rex Boynton, SAF retail division director, and Herb Mitchell, founder and president of Herb Mitchell Associates. AFS sales vice president Fred Poland told the overflow crowd of florists how they could use AFS as "a profit-making wire service."[15]

Mitchell remembered the early days of his relationship with Herman and presenting the idea of using publications to make AFS a household word among florists. Mitchell was a pioneer in floral industry publications and was excited that Herman was totally receptive to producing a monthly magazine. Mitchell spent a lot of time at Herman's house developing ideas.

AFS sales representatives gave Herman a grandfather clock for his office in 1982. At left is regional sales manager Larry Fassler.

He said, "Herman is a visionary. He knows where he wants to go. I never once talked to Herman when he did not have some direction in mind. He always knew there was opportunity and his goal was how do we get there."[16]

Herman used the word "consistency" to explain to potential subscribers why they should choose AFS over the competition. Herman believed that AFS offered consistent ownership, management, rebates, and service, unlike the other floral wire services in the nation.[17]

In September, 1981, AFS conducted its most successful sales effort ever. On the Tuesday after the Labor Day weekend, the company used phone banks set up at the Myriad Convention Center in downtown Oklahoma City in an all-out blitz of the country's florists to try to add new AFS members. Basil Holt remembered, "For two weeks, we made calls from daylight to dark, beginning on the east coast and working our way across the United States each day."[18]

The florists contacted were on a list that Herman had been keeping for years—a list of florists who he thought would make good subscribers, but for some reason had not yet joined AFS. The list had grown to 12,000, making it necessary for every sales representative at AFS to work phone lines that did not go silent until Alaska and Hawaii had shut down each evening. The blitz was incredibly successful—more than 3,300 new florists were added to the growing AFS subscriber list.[19]

There were a few lighter moments during the blitz. Barry Bernstein saw Herman walking toward his area while monitoring calls being made by AFS employees. Bernstein pretended Herman was not there and said to an imaginary florist, "Mrs. Jones, yes, I understand your husband has just had a heart attack and is on the way to the hospital, but more importantly, I have a special offer from AFS that you need to know about."[20]

Herman used sales methods during the blitz he had learned selling margarine at the grocery store in Tampa, Florida, years before. Herman saw each call as an opportunity to sell a new member several ads in upcoming directories.

"Limiting" the number of ads that could be bought had the same lure as limiting the number of pounds of margarine

Wired For Customer Satisfaction

The Image Of Your Shop Is Often Judged By How You Handle A Wire Order.

a grocery store customer could buy. An AFS marketing representative would typically say, "Since you are a member now, you are eligible to buy an ad in the directory, but the limit is five." Often, the eager customer immediately purchased five ads and began asking if an exception could be made for his floral shop. The salesman's response was always, "Well, if you go above five, we have to talk to Herman." Going to the top of the company for authority increased ad sales tremendously.[21]

"The blitz solidified both the employees of AFS and the company's reputation around the nation," Basil Holt remembers. "It showed we meant business and were interested in a personal relationship with our subscribers."[22]

The 1981 blitz was a benchmark in AFS history. Bob Meinders was all for the project but recognized that a huge cash investment had to be made to print and mail promotional kits, rent space at the Oklahoma City convention center, and obtain dozens of phone lines. Bob later said, "It was a major, major expense, but it was a tremendous payoff."[23]

In the fall of 1981, Jim Morley joined AFS as director

of special projects and Jake Vanbebber became the company's credit manager. The latest AFS directory grew from 1,415 pages in a three-column format to 1,451 pages in a four-column format. The **37 percent growth** was a direct result of the Labor Day blitz.

Morley's addition to the staff increased AFS efforts to provide educational opportunities for member florists. Morley, a veteran floral designer and former president of the Missouri State Florists Association, immediately began producing design schools. The first successful event was a school at the Galleria in Houston, Texas, featuring innovative visual effects to illustrate designs and trends in weddings. Within a few months, in the spring of 1982, Morley took his design school on the road with programs at conventions in Michigan and Florida. The audio-visual presentation at Michigan State University, where Morley had first learned about flowers while taking a short course in horticulture, was a huge success, attended by 1,200 florists and designers.[24]

Soon, florists in packed convention halls were introduced to dazzling, professionally produced audio and visual presentations on subjects ranging from "Let's Design a Wedding" to "Fundamentals of Telephone Selling."

Morley enjoyed having Herman present at AFS educational events. "His pleasant attitude and phenomenal memory made Herman a drawing card," Morley said. "If he met a florist, he not only remembered their shop, but also could talk about a good restaurant within a half block of the shop. People loved him."[25]

As another service to florists, AFS published the *Professional Floral Designer*, a publication devoted entirely to professional floral design. Herb Mitchell was editor-in-chief and Eulalah Overmeyher was managing editor of the publication. Contributing articles to the intitial issues of the magazine were Dennis Buttelwerth, Haskell Eargle, Joe Gordy, Michael Polychrones, and Jack Schneider, all members of the prestigious American Institute of Floral Designers. Over the years, many AIFD designers contributed to the magazine.

Mitchell saw Herman as a patient man, especially in

putting together a world-class educational program for florists. Mitchell said Herman was like the shepherd who got all his 35 sheep to the top of the mountain one by one, while another shepherd was still trying to herd the entire flock at one time. Mitchell said, "Other people thought Herman was impatient, but that is not true. Herman was willing to get one sheep at a time up the mountain."[26]

Even though AFS was growing in sales volume and number of employees, the company was still run like a family operation. It was not uncommon for Herman to stop by a local bar to play pool and shuffleboard with employees who were winding down after a tough week. Donna Corjay remembered, "He never stayed long, but when he left, he always paid the employees' bar bill."[27]

Employees enjoyed chili cook-offs, bicycle races, talent shows, road rallies, luaus, monthly catered lunches, and many parties to solidify their friendship and goal of making AFS a successful company.

On one occasion, a major ice storm, and the resulting automobile accidents, closed roads and highways. Corjay said, "Herman piled the employees into his car and drove many miles in different directions to deliver them home safely. If he couldn't get around a car, he drove in the median."[28]

Herman also cared about his employees' personal problems. He once loaned $500 to a young man whose wife had left him with two small boys under the age of three and needed the advance for childcare and to pay insurance premiums.[29]

A New Home Office

CHAPTER 9

THE SOLID GROWTH OF AFS WAS THE RESULT OF
HERMAN SETTING THE EXAMPLE OF HARD
WORK AND DEDICATION.
ROBERT H. MEINDERS

Just more than a decade old, AFS was establishing its place in the American floral industry. In addition to being a clearinghouse for floral orders that guaranteed payment to florists filling orders, AFS offered many optional services such as design and management training to improve the efficiency, profitability, and professionalism of member florists. An early promotional brochure stated, "We will stay flexible and adapt to meet the challenges of an ever-changing marketplace. AFS will continue to develop valuable services that will strengthen the bond between hometown AFS florists and their customers."[1]

As florist Walter Metz observed, "Herman had an advantage over other CEO's of wire services. He knew that florists were among the hardest working people in America because he had seen them all in action—he had walked in their shoes. He knew what they needed to survive and make a profit."[2]

Herman also was aware of territorial boundaries in the floral business. Jim Morley said, "He would not sell items such as containers directly to retail florists—because that would infringe upon the sales territory of wholesalers. He had respect for

everyone in the industry—and they reciprocated with their loyalty and their business."[3] Herman had become a household name in the floral industry. Frances Dudley, publisher of the industry's oldest publication, *Florist Review,* remembered the moment she first met Herman at a convention. Someone whis-

Herman and daughter, Kathy.

pered, "Herman's in the room," as Dudley entered a convention reception. She said, "He commanded tremendous respect simply by his presence."[4]

Katrina Holloway, a wholesale florist from Texas, liked Herman because he was such a "people person."[5] She said, "It wouldn't make any difference if you were the president of the United States or owner of a tiny flower shop in West Texas, if you approached Herman, he knew instantly who you were, called you by name, and was the most gracious person you ever met."[6]

Education of florists soon became the hallmark of the success of AFS. While FTD was still the industry leader and paid

Left: **Christy Meinders on her fifth birthday.** *Below:* **Herman and daughter, Christy.**

for much national advertising, AFS decided to use design schools and seminars to get its message out to the nation's florists.

Herman's belief that education was the key to promoting AFS grew out of his strong relationship with floral wholesalers who needed designers and commentators to assist in their presentations to retailers. Being around wholesalers so much allowed Herman to know what florists wanted. He said, "If the wholesalers said do something, the retailers fell in line. Many times, wholesalers gave us leads and became some of our best sales people."[7]

AFS put together the nation's most qualified team of designers and commentators to appear at wholesalers' shows.

Herman said, "We began to get the best shows at the best times in the best locations around the country, all of which made AFS the education leader."[8]

The emphasis on education was also driven by a cost factor. AFS did not have the money to compete with FTD in national advertising or in creating products. However, AFS designers and commentators accomplished much more with florists than just introducing a new product. One-on-one conversations at seminars and schools created trust and confidence in AFS. Herman remembered, "Rather than competing head-to-head with FTD, we went a different direction and created our own avenue of reaching florists."[9]

Herman had another way of expressing his theory about sponsoring floral design seminars and providing commentators at conventions—it was better to spend a dollar to get ten dollars worth of publicity than to spend ten dollars and only get ten dollars worth.[10]

By knowing so many florists at every level of the floral industry, Herman was able to develop a support system for them all—wholesalers, retailers, designers, and manufacturers. Florists appreciated the support of AFS and demonstrated their appreciation by using AFS as their wire service of choice.

Herman used exotic annual convention sites to lure customers away from FTD. AFS could not compete with FTD in spending hundreds of thousands of dollars in renting a huge convention center and staffing it to produce a national convention. However, by holding conventions on cruise ships, AFS was

A.F.S.'s extra profit rebate for 1981 could exceed $1,250,000.00.

Are you getting your share?

An envelope stuffer mailed in monthly statements to florists promoted the AFS rebate program.

Even though American Floral Services was only ten years old in 1980, Herman had become a leader in the American floral industry. When florists said the name, "Herman," everyone knew who they were talking about. *Facing page:* Christy Meinders' photograph appeared on the cover of an AFS brochure announcing new rebates for participating florists.

able to obtain many convention services without cost. For example, if AFS could guarantee several hundred members would buy tickets for the cruise, the ship provided free meeting rooms and other services that would have cost hard cash if the convention was held elsewhere.

A secondary benefit of holding conventions on cruise ships was the bragging that customers did for the next few months. Rather than talking to their competitors about attending a drab convention in some distant city, florists might display photographs of their trips with AFS on board a romantic cruise ship. After all, one of television's most popular programs of the time was *The Love Boat.*

Herman not only was committed to his own company, he cared for and supported many national and international floral organizations. He made himself, and his checkbook, available to the Society of American Florists, the American Institute of Floral Designers, and state floral groups throughout the country. He later became president or chairman of many of the organizations of which he was a member.

The Society of American Florists (SAF) was uniquely

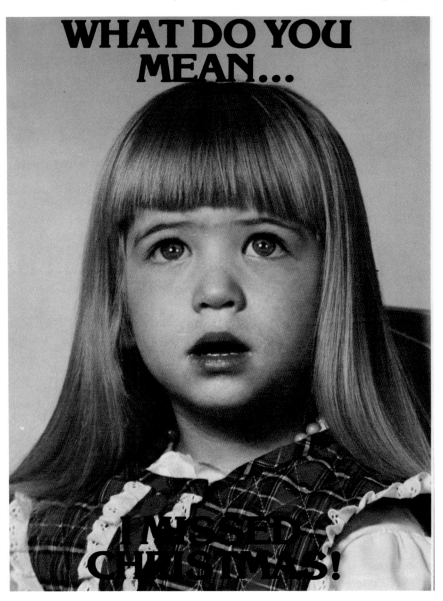

Left: Herman in his office at AFS headquarters on Northwest 36th Street in Oklahoma City in 1981. *Below:* Bob Meinders was vice president of finance and treasurer of AFS. One of his most enjoyable tasks each month was to oversee the computer operation that sent extra profit rebate checks to AFS florists.

created by an act of Congress in 1884 and represented all segments of the floral industry—retail florists, wholesalers, importers, suppliers, and growers. One of SAF's major functions was to represent the floral industry in Washington, D.C.—to make certain the executive and legislative branches of the federal government understood the impact proposed legislation would have on the industry.

Peter Moran, the CEO of SAF, worked closely with Herman in developing a strategy for the organization. Herman became chairman of the SAF Government Relations Committee. Moran remembered, "Herman was careful to know where SAF's influence should be used. He also was very respectful of everyone in the industry—he would never use our organization to promote government action that would help one segment—and hurt another."[11]

In a membership drive for SAF, Herman encouraged his AFS sales representatives to sell memberships in SAF, creating several thousand new members for that organization. The idea was the brainchild of then SAF president Del Demaree, Jr., who said, "Herman always said yes to any project SAF

Above: **Tom Petuskey was credit manager and head of the subscription committee at AFS in 1981. Later, Petuskey was elected court clerk of Oklahoma County.**
Right: **Western regional sales manager Larry Fassler, vice president of sales Fred Poland, and Eastern regional sales manager Darrell Lake headed up the sales organization.**

unveiled that would benefit the floral industry." Demaree was president of Syndicate Sales, the industry's largest manufacturer and distributor of floral products.[12]

AFS also gave $55,000 to SAF to help build a new Center for Commercial Floriculture in Arlington, Virginia.

Herman cared about the plight of his subscribers, especially when they were caught in an economic downturn or needed additional funds for a special project. Lynn Lary McLean, a florist in Friendswood, Texas, remembered a time when officials of the Texas State Floral Association ran short of funds to complete the construction of a new building. When McLean and others presented the problem to Herman, he loaned the association the money to continue with the project. McLean remembered, "Herman asked no questions because he believed in us, wanted to support us in any way, and knew we would pay the money back."[13]

Herman was also involved with the American Floral Endowment (AFE), a non-profit organization that primarily funds floral research and education programs at various colleges and universities in the United States. Eventually, Herman gave substantial funds to the group and served for many years as chairman and trustee. Bob Carbone, a wholesale florist from Cranston, Rhode Island, worked with Herman on AFE projects. Carbone said, "He was unique in the detail that he wanted to make a project work. He wanted every "i" dotted and every "t" crossed. He is a unique thinker, but his attention to detail defies the imagination."[14]

By the early 1980s, AFS had growing pains. Now handling more than two million orders a year with 76 employees, the company was running out of space. AFS had occupied its home office at 3716 Northwest 36th Street since 1976. In early 1982, Herman, Bob, and their management team approved plans for a new million dollar building to be constructed at 3737 Northwest 34th Street, on a lot directly south of the office.

Although Herman hired an architect and contractor for the project, he kept a close watch to ensure the building was built to his specifications. The contractor assured Herman the building would be completed by September 30. The contractor

In February, 1982, Eulalah Overmeyer, holding a framed citation, and her husband, Bob, seated at right, were honored on their 50th wedding anniversary at a celebration at Oklahoma City's Hilton Inn. Eulalah was known as the "First Lady of the Floral Industry." Her contributions to the success of AFS's education programs were immeasurable.

had other projects, and Herman noticed that fewer workers began showing up to work on the AFS structure. Daily conversations with the contractor did not satisfy Herman that the completion deadline would be met.

The situation came to a head on Wednesday, October 7, 1982, when Herman informed the contractor that AFS would move into the building the following Saturday. The contractor replied, "You can't! It won't be ready yet!"

Construction workers were astonished the following Monday morning when they saw that the building was occupied by AFS employees. The move had taken place over the weekend, even though there was little carpet on the floors, several walls were yet to be painted, and many other finishing touches were lacking.[15]

When the contractor asked Herman for an explanation, Herman said, "You're late and you have no good reason for the delay. I told you last Wednesday that we were moving. Now, you can finish the project by working around us, but not during our business hours."[16]

The contractor dispatched a full crew to the site to work 24 hours a day to complete the building as soon as possible, before the employees were further settled into their offices.

The fourth move for AFS was a giant leap from the garage apartment in which the company began 12 years before. The new three-story, 43,000-square-foot facility was needed to house growing staff and a new Hewlett Packard Series 44 computer system called Huey 1. The new computer had 20 times more auxiliary storage and 15 times more order processing power than the previous system.[17]

On November 20, 1982, candlelight and soft music greeted more than 500 guests from the United States and Canada

Right: **The new AFS logo was unveiled in 1983.** *Below:* **The new AFS headquarters building was officially opened on November 20, 1982. It was a gala occasion at which Herman and company officials hosted more than 500 guests from the floral industry.**

at the grand opening of the new AFS headquarters. State Senator Mike Combs joined Society of American Florists President Del Demaree, Herman, and Bob Meinders in cutting the ribbon to officially dedicate the building.

At the dedication, Herman gave full credit to AFS employees for the success of the company and increasing the number of subscribers to more than 15,000.

Above: **Herman, center, at the World Flower Council summit in Hong Kong in 1982.** *Below:* **Herman supported the World Flower Council with both his time and money. Left to right, at the WFC mini-summit meeting in Seoul, South Korea, are Aida Martinez, Mexico; Alice Lin, China; Helen Blakey, Canada; Herman, representing the United States; Sim K. Soon, South Korea; and Yaga Shita, Japan.**

The new headquarters was a dream come true for Herman. The building featured a spectacular entrance area. A recessed entryway, paved in brick, led to a pair of 15-foot ebony doors. The elegant atmosphere of the lobby continued throughout the building. Bright red enameled doors opened into Herman's presidential suite.

Herman had a close brush with death in 1982. His mother, who had moved to Oklahoma City, died and Herman took the responsibility of taking her body home to Minnesota for burial next to her husband, who had passed away in 1972. He leased a private plane to fly into the municipal airport in Pipestone. In a heavy fog just before landing, the plane hit something. Immediately, Herman thought surely the aircraft had collided with a tree, a silo, or

Above: Dean White, a long-time AFS member florist, who succeeded Herman as Chairman of the World Flower Council. *Right:* Paul Goodman, a former vice president of Florafax, owned *Floral Finance* and developed the Rosebud computer software program to help florists.

television tower. The pilot, Clarence Taylor, maintained control of the aircraft, although he and Herman thought they could possibly crash.

The danger was averted and they landed safely. There was no way to determine exactly what the airplane hit, but aviation officials guessed the plane may have hit a huge Canadian goose. Whatever they collided with, the incident shook Herman up. When he arrived at the motel where his brother, Bob, was staying, he began sobbing. Bob remembered, "We were both in tears and probably looked at life a little differently after that day."[18]

Settled into new offices, AFS branched out into the world flower industry in 1983. The company established a state-of-the-art AFS Education Center at the new office complex. The first AFS Commentators Seminar was held in February, 1983.

Herman, left, presents a peace pipe, made from pipestone from his hometown in Minnesota, to Chung Lee, the president of Taiwan, during a floral convention in Taipei.

New audiovisual programs, "Basic to High Style," "Show and Sell...with Pizzazzle," and "Hooked on Flowers," were made available to florists.

Herman and his staff strongly supported Japanese florist Jazaburo Sekiye in producing the first Pan Pacific Flower Culture Conference in Gifu and Tokyo, Japan, in May, 1983. The group later changed its name to the World Flower Council (WFC).

AFS leadership in the floral industry was recognized in 1984 when Herman was elected vice chairman of the World Flower Council, the new name given by Herman and Jazaburo Sekiye, right, to the organization formerly known as the Pan Pacific Flower Culture Conference. AFS director of special events Jim Morley was elected president of the American Institute of Floral Designers, another indication that AFS was becoming a strong voice in the world of flowers.

Continuing the international flavor, the AFS international convention was held in the Orient in 1983. Convention delegates attended the Pan Pacific event, toured Japanese schools and wholesale auction houses, and visited factories, flower shops, and experimental farms in Hong Kong. A post-convention tour to mainland China topped off the exciting convention.

During the next two decades, the WFC held conferences in Hawaii, Australia, The Netherlands, Japan, Taiwan, South Korea, Las Vegas, Canada, Spain, Hong Kong, South Africa, Malaysia, Russia, Italy, Thailand, The Philippines, and Latvia.

Major promotions were made within the company in 1983 as a new telemarketing department came on line and a new color wheel, a first for the industry, was distributed to florists. Donna Corjay was named director of personnel and Mark Nance became national sales manager.

Nance, a business school graduate of the University of Oklahoma, was hired after extensive interviews with Herman and his brother, Bob. It was Herman who called Nance to convince him that AFS was the place to be for the future. Nance said, "Herman was maybe the best salesman I ever met. He convinced me I would be making a mistake if I moved out of state and took another job." Once hired, Nance was immediately sent to a sales convention in Acapulco, Mexico, to take charge of the national sales force.[19]

In another move to help florists succeed financially, AFS began offering *Floral Finance,* a monthly publication owned by Paul Goodman, a former vice president and general manager of Florafax, who had a Master of Business Administration degree from Stanford University. Herman and Goodman recognized that many small floral shops needed help to understand financial statements and banking transactions. Goodman literally pioneered the idea of providing financial help to florists.[20]

When the *Floral Finance* newsletter was only a few months old, Goodman offered a computer software package to florists. The idea was revolutionary because personal computers were still a luxury for most small businesses. However, Goodman

developed the
Rosebud soft-
ware program
that allowed flo-
rists to comput-
erize bookkeep-
ing and order
tracking. The
first three pur-
chasers of the Rosebud program were Jane Knox and Bob Hardy
in Texas and Mary Lee Evans in Tulsa, Oklahoma.[21]

Even though *Floral Finance* was financially backed by
AFS, and later absorbed into the company, it was still considered
a separate entity, allowing Goodman to rent booth space at the
FTD annual convention in Hawaii. Goodman remembered, "It
was an exciting time, giving the little guy a chance to have a
computer in his business."[22]

With Herman's backing, Goodman became a "mis-
sionary" to florists with his message that better financial records
could allow retailers to make wiser business decisions and ultimately create more profitable shops.

In January, 1984, the AFS Center for Advanced Floral
Training held its first seminar. The first year's schedule was so
successful there was a waiting list for each session. Students from
many states and Canada attended the Commentators and Com-
munication Seminar held at the home office in February, 1984.

Letting Go of the Reins

CHAPTER 10

HARDLY ANYONE BELIEVED THAT HERMAN
WOULD GRADUALLY STEP BACK AND ALLOW
SOMEONE ELSE TO RUN THE COMPANY HE
FOUNDED. AFTER ALL, IT WAS HIS BABY.
TOM BUTLER

In the years of unprecedented growth of AFS, Herman
depended greatly upon his brother, Bob. While Herman was the
entrepreneur and expert salesman, Bob was strong in dealing
with other staff members and making certain the financial side of
the company was healthy. Each year, AFS experienced phenomenal growth as more florists began taking advantage of rebates
and quality service offered by AFS.

But by 1984, Herman realized his company was so
large, he was no longer a one-man show as leader of the fastest-
growing floral wire service in the world. He spent a lot of time
thinking about his future and the future of AFS. Should he sell
the business? Should he allow AFS to become a public company?

After all, it had become fashionable for family-owned businesses to go public and the owners retire with unheard-of sums of cash.

Herman read a book titled *Going Public,* distributed by Arthur Andersen & Co. It is interesting to review the sections of the book that Herman highlighted with a yellow marker. He was obviously concerned with the book's advice on how to select a managing underwriter for a public offering of stock, the housekeeping items that were necessary before a privately owned company went public, and the timetable for a public offering. The yellow highlighting mysteriously stops halfway through the book when Herman came to the part of the book that predicted that it could cost $400,000 to take a company public. No doubt, austere-thinking Herman quickly lost interest in going public.

There was another reason why Herman was skeptical about AFS becoming a publicly-owned company. He thought far beyond his own personal well being—he was genuinely concerned about how any action he would take would affect his employees who had been loyal and productive even during less than profitable times.

He was also concerned that future AFS management treat his longtime, loyal customers properly. Many of his customers, like Mildred Riddle of Midland, Texas, had been original subscribers, and were like family members. When Riddle went through a long illness, it was not unusual for her to receive an occasional phone call of encouragement from Herman. She said, "In what other business would the owner of the company call, concerned about my health?"[1]

After considering several people to take his place as president of AFS, Herman convinced Tom Butler to join the company, with a long range plan for him to eventually lead the company. Butler had been in the floral industry since 1969. He worked at FTD for years with the goal of someday becoming president of a floral wire service. He assumed that goal would be accomplished at FTD.

A native of Detroit, Michigan, Butler attended a Catholic seminary in training for the priesthood. However, he taught English and journalism at a Catholic high school in

Herman and Tom Butler, right, a 16-year veteran of the floral industry, who became president of AFS in October, 1985. Butler had worked for many years for AFS's chief rival, FTD.

Detroit before joining FTD where he ascended the corporate ladder to advertising editor and director of the huge wire service's international division. His plans to lead that company were derailed when he took a job with a major floral products wholesaler, Syndicate Sales.

Herman had known Butler for years and was surprised to see him in 1982 at a trade fair in Atlanta. Herman told Butler, "I can't believe you have left FTD. I just assumed you would be president someday." Herman told Butler, "If I had known you were leaving FTD, I would have wanted to talk to you about our company." Butler had made a commitment to Syndicate and did not seriously entertain any possible move to AFS.

In April, 1985, Richard Milteer was conducting an education seminar at the AFS home office. While discussing the company with Milteer, Herman mentioned that he really needed to bring someone on board to assume a leadership role. Milteer suggested Herman consider Butler because Butler had done a great job at FTD and had always wanted to run a wire service.

Following Milteer's advice, Herman called Butler the following morning with an invitation to meet sometime to talk about Herman's plans for the future of AFS. Butler first talked to his wife, Jo, and then called Herman back. The two met the following day in Oklahoma City. After touring the offices and meeting some of the AFS personnel, Butler and Herman talked. Butler assumed that Herman wanted him to run one of the divisions of the company and was shocked when Herman said, "Tom, I need someone to run the whole company."

Butler assumed Herman's brother, Bob, would want to run AFS. However, to prove otherwise, Herman picked up the phone and dialed Bob's extension. Bob confirmed the fact that he was not interested in becoming president of AFS.

Within minutes, Herman convinced Butler to come to AFS for one year as executive vice president to see if he was interested in becoming president, and if Herman was satisfied that he was the man for the job. There was no contract or days of dealings with lawyers—Herman and Butler simply shook hands. That was okay with Butler, who remembered, "I knew Herman's reputation in the industry and that his word was better than any written contract."

Butler worked closely with Herman in running the day-to-day operations of the company and developing long range plans and goals for AFS. Just six months after Butler arrived, Herman brought him into his office one day and announced, "I know we said one year, but I'm happy, and if you're happy, let's just make you president now." Butler agreed and, in typical

Herman and LaDonna Meinders became good friends with Jo and Tom Butler as Tom took over more responsibility of running the day-to-day operations of AFS.

Herman Meinders fashion, the transfer of leadership happened overnight. Butler was the new president and Herman became chairman of the board of AFS.

In announcing the change to employees on October 1, 1985, Herman said, "In the time Tom has been here, I have worked closely with him and found him to be uniquely qualified to step into the role as president. He proves his dedication to AFS florists and to the floral industry every day."[2]

Few people believed that Herman would actually turn over the reins of AFS to someone else—after all, he had founded the company that was now making a huge impact on the floral industry. However, Herman had confidence in Butler and became less involved in the daily operations as each year passed. Instead, Herman spent more time promoting the floral industry and was able to become more involved in community affairs and giving back to the city and state where his business had flourished.

"Even though Herman turned over the presidency of the company," remembered AFS vice president of finance, Tony Lovio, "you could still feel his presence."[3] Herman still insisted on AFS employees answering the phone within three rings, part of AFS's commitment to true service to member florists, and to never argue with a customer.[4]

As president, Butler continued Herman's idea of emphasizing support services for member florists. The company supplied subscribers with comprehensive advertising packages that included window banners designed to capture the attention of passersby; ad slicks and radio scripts, ready for use in local newspapers and on radio stations; care tags to brighten arrangements; and posters announcing coming holidays which should be celebrated with the giving of flowers. AFS sent a steady stream of promotional items to florists—promoting everything from National Mother-in-Law's Day to National Secretary's Day.

In 1985, AFS introduced the AFS Americom Worldwide Telecommunications Network, a new system that made sending wire orders more efficient. Under the plan, an AFS subscriber could purchase computer hardware for less than $1,000 and use the speedier and more reliable electronic communication system created by General Electric.

The concept of florists sending orders electronically revolutionized the industry. Today, Teleflora's Dove Network, a prodigy of AFS's original system, electronically connects more than 20,000 florists who send tens of thousands of wire orders daily. During high order times, the volume can grow to more than 250,000 orders in a single day.

Herman saw the value of using computers in the floral industry, even though he could not adapt to the new world of computers himself. Rather than use a word processor, he continued to hand-write notes that later would be typed by his secretary, Evelyn Chappell.

AFS continued to expand its seminar and audiovisual programs and supported regional and national floral design

The 1985 AFS sales staff. At the front of the group are Herman, left, and new AFS president, Tom Butler.

competitions. Director of special projects, Jim Morley, coordinated the Great American Design Contest for florists both in the United States and Canada.

By the end of 1985, AFS had 17,275 florists. In early 1986, the company increased its order rebate program with the introduction of the Ad-Vantage Rebate. Florists received a $1.00 rebate on orders up to 499 each month and $1.50 for each order if the florist exceeded 500 orders on the monthly statement.

In just 16 years, AFS had grown to serve more than 18,000 florists and customers in 22,000 cities and most foreign countries.

LaDonna, in a gown given her by Mrs. John A. Brown, who, with her husband, owned a famous Oklahoma City department store. The gown was part of LaDonna's wardrobe for the Miss America pageant.

LaDonna

CHAPTER 11

WHEN HERMAN MARRIED LADONNA, HIS LIFE
OPENED UP-IT LIT UP. THERE WAS A VOID THAT HE
COULD NOT FILL WITHOUT HER.
PETE GARCIA

LaDonna Jane Kramer was born August 16, 1936.
She grew up on a windswept wheat farm along the Cimarron
River near Loyal in Kingfisher County, Oklahoma. Her family
had a rich heritage in northwest Oklahoma. Her grandfather,
Henry Kramer, emigrated from Germany and settled in what
would become Kingfisher County shortly after Oklahoma Territory was created by congressional action.

The Kramers were among many German immigrants
to settle in this part of Oklahoma Territory. Some of the families
had lived together briefly near Palatine, Illinois. LaDonna's
great-great-uncle, Dr. Paul Friedemann, set up a medical practice
in the village that grew up around wheat farms in Kingfisher
County. He applied for a post office and officially named the
community Kiel, after a town in Germany. However, during
World War I, citizens of Kiel, in a show of loyalty to the United

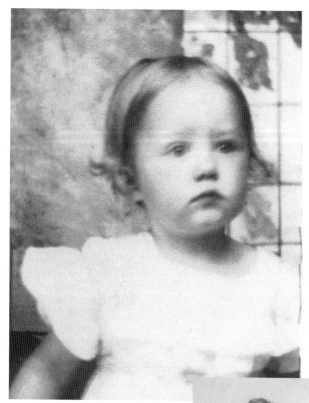

States, renamed the town Loyal. When LaDonna was small, it was not uncommon for old timers to announce they were going to Kiel on Saturday.[1]

LaDonna's father, Ewald Julius "E.J." Kramer, was adopted by his aunt and uncle and grew up in a German-speaking family. He took his first job in Shawnee, Oklahoma, at a lumber company. In Shawnee, he met Alma Smith and

Above: LaDonna Jane Kramer was born in 1936 in Okeene, Oklahoma, and grew up on the family farm in Kingfisher County. *Right:* LaDonna, right, slept in the same bed with her older sister, Ruth Evelyn, left, until they were teenagers. They shared everything, from toys to chores.

E.J. Kramer and Alma Smith, while dating in 1929. Two years later, they were married.

they were married in 1931. When Mr. Kramer lost his job in 1932 in the Great Depression, he and his wife moved to the family farm in Kingfisher County.

LaDonna's first memories of her father were of him working long hours preparing the soil for another wheat crop, and threshing the wheat during harvest. Mr. Kramer was true to his conservative German ancestry and believed in honesty and hard work—a combination that made his agricultural efforts successful. His tall and lean frame cast a huge shadow for LaDonna and her older sister, Ruth Evelyn. He loved to wear patched and re-patched overalls, although he dutifully put on his suit to attend services at the Loyal Evangelical and Reformed Church each Sunday morning.[2]

LaDonna's mother also came from a long line of hard-

Above: E.J. and Alma Kramer on their 60th wedding anniversary, August 1, 1991, with the same 1929 Whippet roadster in which they courted. LaDonna, who now owns the car, placed the "Just Married" sign in the window of the car for the anniversary celebration on the Kramer home place.

Right: E.J. Kramer with his first great-grandchild, Craig Ode. Mr. Kramer died December 1, 2000, at his home in Kingfisher, Oklahoma.

working farm- ers. Her father, Sterling Price Smith, was born in Missouri during the Civil War. Before his twin brother, Lee, died at age 96, the two were believed to be the oldest living identical twins in the nation. Alma was not

German, a fact that did not go unnoticed in the mostly German community in which they lived. However, her household skills equaled those of any of her German neighbors.[3]

LaDonna grew up knowing that the family fortunes depended each year upon nature and the world commodity market over which her parents had no control. In a 1989 book about her childhood, *Leaves In The Wind,* LaDonna wrote, "Agriculture is a business of faith, and a crop in the field is a fragile commodity against the forces of nature. Many years, we saw the crop and all our hopes disappear during one brief spring hail-storm. Other years, drought and green bugs did their damage."[4]

LaDonna had a wonderful childhood with a loving family. She and her older sister took advantage of long days in the summer, playing outside as late as they could. The northwestern Oklahoma sun baked the roof of the family home that was cooled only with an oscillating fan blowing air over a pan of ice cubes. It was a treat for the family when the old hand-crank ice cream freezer was pulled down from its place in the shed and filled with rich ingredients that soon turned into homemade ice cream.[5]

Winters could be as harsh as summers in Kingfisher County. LaDonna's father cut firewood from the canyons near their house. When she was small, LaDonna helped drive a team of horses into the bottom land to pull a load of firewood back to the house. On cold nights, the family sat around the wood stove and dared not close the door to the bedrooms, taking advantage of the heat that emanated from the hot coals all night. Some-times, Mrs. Kramer would heat bricks on the wood stove and wrap them in blankets to place in the girls' bed. On the coldest nights, a glass of water sitting by the bed would freeze by daylight.[6]

LaDonna's father was extra careful about the condi-tion of his wood stove, because the Kramer house had burned when LaDonna was nine months old. However, Mr. Kramer paid $250 for a house on a farm three miles east of Loyal and moved it to his land. The house had once been occupied by the Walton family, whose son, Sam, left Kingfisher County and eventually founded Wal-Mart and became one of the richest men in the world.[7]

LaDonna, left, as Miss Oklahoma, helped celebrate the semi-centennial of her home state in 1957 by assisting the outgoing Miss Oklahoma, Ann Campbell, apply a semi-centennial bumper sticker on the car of Oklahoma Governor Raymond Gary. *Courtesy Oklahoma Publishing Company.*

LaDonna, like most children of farm families, enjoyed the bounty of the land—baskets of vegetables from the garden and home cured beef. After the vegetables were harvested each year, LaDonna, her sister, and mother spent hours canning in the kitchen. LaDonna remembered, "Canning was serious and systematic." Last year's fruit jars were retrieved from the basement, then washed and scalded. Peaches, LaDonna's favorite item to be canned, and other foods for the coming winter were preserved in the jars.[8]

The Kramer girls wore homemade clothing to the local school, a two-story red brick building at the east edge of Loyal. LaDonna loved her teachers and her classes. Later, she was an active member of the local 4-H Club and participated in sewing, canning, gardening, and home improvement projects.

Even though they were two years apart, LaDonna and Ruth Evelyn were very close. They shared a room and bed, toys, and even chores. Sometimes the girls rode a pony to get the mail at the family mailbox that was located more than a mile from their house.

The girls were very different. LaDonna said, "Ruth Evelyn had a passion for orderliness that I never experienced. I lost things, she saved them. I played with my dolls, dressing and undressing them, combing their hair, painting their poor mouths with nail polish, and wearing them out with love...Ruth Evelyn played with her dolls carefully and loved them with reserve." When Ruth Evelyn outgrew dolls and packed them away, their hair was still neatly combed and their dresses looked like new.[9]

LaDonna's love for music probably began while following along with words of hymns at the Evangelical and Reformed Church in Loyal as soon as she could read. She began taking piano lessons from a neighbor at age five and her first recital was in the summer before fifth grade.

LaDonna became a serious music student, often practicing piano two or three hours a day and studying under a Bethany Nazarene College student, David Uerkvitz, who came to Kingfisher to teach on Saturdays. On the day she turned 16, LaDonna began teaching piano in Kingfisher, taking over Uerkvitz's class of 16 students after he graduated from college and moved away.

Soon, LaDonna began taking lessons from Jewel Major Roche, an accomplished teacher in Oklahoma City. It was not an easy task to get to lessons. LaDonna drove to Kingfisher, took a bus to Oklahoma City, and then traveled to Mrs. Roche's house by taxi.[10]

LaDonna's parents allowed her to move to Oklahoma City for her senior year in high school and live with Mrs. Roche. It was a cultural shock to move from a class of 16 students at Loyal to a class of nearly 600 at Classen High School. However, the experience was rich for LaDonna as she was introduced to symphonies and musical productions and learned about living in a large city.

LaDonna continued her musical training at Oklahoma City University under the watchful eye of Dr. Clarence Burg, a revered pianist and music teacher and dean of the OCU School of Music. LaDonna blossomed musically—she became an accomplished pianist, was introduced to all kinds of music,

and sang in the OCU choir.[11]

She was not only talented, but beautiful, an observation proved by her se-

Top: **LaDonna and Ellen Jayne Wheeler, left, performed duo piano concerts to audiences all over Oklahoma. Their performances were sponsored by the Oklahoma Arts Council. In 1976, their concert tour took them to the Kennedy Center in Washington, D.C., as part of the Bicentennial Celebration.** *Center:* **LaDonna and her three sons—left to right, Mark Gooden, Joe Gooden, and John Gooden, on Joe's 25th birthday.** *Below:* **John Gooden and his family at their Kingfisher home in 2001. Left to right, John, Aaron, Jody, and Valerie.**

Above: Three generations—left to right, Lori Gooden Ode, LaDonna's daughter; Alma Kramer, LaDonna's mother; and LaDonna. *Right:* LaDonna's daughter, Lori, married Chris Ode, left. In this 1995 photograph in Hawaii, Lori is holding daughter, Alexandra, and son Craig is in front.

lection as Oklahoma Maid of Cotton in her sophomore year. Growing up in wheat country, LaDonna knew little about Oklahoma's cotton industry before she entered the contest in November, 1955, and posed for publicity shots on huge, white bales of cotton.

With the experience of the Maid of Cotton competition behind her, LaDonna, as Miss Kingfisher, entered the Miss Oklahoma pageant held in

Above: **Mark Gooden and his family. Left to right, stepson Stark Kremeier; Stark's fiancé, Jennifer Poteet; Mark; his wife, Regina; and stepson Michael Kremeier.** *Left:* **LaDonna with grandchildren, left to right, Valerie, Aaron, Alexandra, Craig, and Michael.**

Oklahoma City in July, 1956. She spent the early summer at home, helping with farm chores and diligently practicing her piano selection, Liszt's "Etude in D-Flat."

In a magical moment, LaDonna was announced as the winner and became Miss Oklahoma for 1956, a term that lasted until July, 1957, a special year because of the state's semi-centennial celebration. While preparing for the Miss America competition in Atlantic City, New Jersey, *The Daily Oklahoman* sent a reporter to the Kramer farm. A two-page spread showed LaDonna driving a tractor—something she had never done in her life—but the photo made great copy.[12]

LaDonna boarded an airplane for the first time when she and her chaperone, Dollie Hoskins, flew to Atlantic City for the Miss America pageant. The rehearsals, parades, and publicity were exciting for the farm girl from Loyal. She later wrote, "Walking out on that long ramp alone, with thousands of cheering spectators in the audience and a battery of lights almost blinding me, was an experience I shall never forget."

LaDonna flawlessly performed her talent selection. However, classical piano was obviously not what the judges were looking for that year. During one of the judges' breakfasts, LaDonna got into a mild argument with judge Dave Garroway about the merits of classical music. The eventual winner of the pageant was Marian McKnight of South Carolina, whose talent presentation was an impersonation of Marilyn Monroe.[13]

In 1957, LaDonna married Bill Gooden. A year later, she graduated from OCU with a bachelor's degree in music. Bill spent a year in the management training program at AT&T and three years as an officer in the United States Air Force. After that, the Goodens returned to Kingfisher to establish a home.

Through the years, LaDonna taught piano to more than 200 students, played the organ at Kingfisher's First Christian Church, and raised her four children, Mark William Gooden, Lori Karen Gooden, John Kramer Gooden, and David Josiah "Joe" Gooden.[14]

After a divorce in 1981, LaDonna went to work for the *Kingfisher County Chronicle* as reporter, photographer, and advertising salesperson. She also wrote a weekly column, "Lifestyles with LaDonna," for the newspaper.

In 1983, LaDonna called OCU President Dr. Jerald Walker to inquire about a job. Walker, who knew LaDonna from her days as a student at the university, offered her one of three positions. LaDonna chose the job as assistant director of graduate admissions. Taking advantage of tuition remission for employees, LaDonna earned her MBA from OCU three years later.

In 1984, LaDonna became director of alumni relations for OCU. Her responsibilities included planning homecoming and other alumni activities and improving relations between the university and alumni. In that regard, she was asked in the spring of 1985 by OCU sports information director Jim Whittaker to ask Herman, as an OCU alum, to make a contribution to provide landscaping around the new Norick art building on campus.[15]

At a breakfast meeting in the president's conference room, LaDonna met Herman for the first time. She recalled "a special moment" as they had a conversation before the meeting at which Herman agreed to fund the landscaping project.

AFS vice president Jim Morley, Rex Rudy, and other AFS employees accompanied Herman to the breakfast meeting. On their way back to the office, Rudy told Herman, "That's the most expensive breakfast we'll ever have—it cost you $50,000, $10,000 a plate!"[16]

In November, 1985, while preparing for homecoming, LaDonna was assigned the task of writing a story for OCU's *Focus* magazine about Herman, who was to receive a Distinguished Alumnus Award from OCU. She went to Herman's office at AFS, received a quick tour of the company headquarters, and went to lunch with him to obtain information about his life. Midway through the interview, Herman asked her to turn off her tape recorder—it made him nervous.[17]

LaDonna enjoyed the conversation with Herman, thinking nothing of his statement that he had been married twice and had no interest in ever getting married again. She never thought about dating him—both were involved in relationships with others.

But fate intervened. Both Herman and LaDonna knew there was something special they felt for each other. At a luncheon honoring Herman, LaDonna switched place cards so she and Herman would be seated together. President Walker announced during the event that singer Vic Damone, whose daughter was a student at OCU, would be giving a concert in a few weeks. Herman and LaDonna talked about what a nice event that would be for OCU.[18]

In a few days, Herman called LaDonna and, during the conversation, she invited him to attend the Damone concert. He eagerly accepted. It was their first date—December 4, 1985.

Within a short time, Herman changed his mind about getting married again. He even visited LaDonna's longtime friend, The Reverend Dr. J. Clyde Wheeler, with questions such as, "How do I get her to marry me?"[19]

During a February, 1986 trip to a floral convention in San Diego, California, Herman formally asked LaDonna to marry him. She accepted and the couple announced plans to be married in June. However, Herman did not want to wait that long and offered to help plan the wedding if the date could be moved up. LaDonna agreed. Dr. Wheeler officiated the ceremony at the OCU Bishop W. Angie Smith Chapel on May 3, 1986.

After a honeymoon in Mexico, LaDonna gave her two weeks' notice to OCU, prompting President Walker to say, "I sent LaDonna out to do a story on Herman Meinders and she never came back."[20]

Herman, right, and his best man, lifelong friend Jack Nessen. Both grew up in Pipestone, Minnesota. Nessen was the reason Herman ended up in Oklahoma City.

LaDonna joined Herman in community involvement and continued her writing. In 1989, she published *Leaves In The Wind*, the story of her childhood in northwest Oklahoma. She was a contributing author of the 1996 book, *365 Meditations for Mothers of Teens*, wrote *Angel Hugs—Heavenly Embraces in Everyday Life* in 2002, and *Angel Hugs for Cancer Patients*, a unique book released in 2004.

Facing Page Above: At LaDonna and Herman's wedding, left to right, Mark William Gooden, John Kramer Gooden, Jody Glazier, LaDonna, Herman, David Josiah "Joe" Gooden, Kathy Meinders, and Lori Karen Gooden. In front is flower girl, Christy Meinders. *Facing Page Left:* LaDonna and Herman were married on the campus of Oklahoma City University May 3, 1986. *Above:* The Meinders grandchildren enjoying Christmas at Herman and LaDonna's home in Oklahoma City. Left to right, Aaron Gooden, Valerie Gooden, Alexandra Ode, and Craig Ode. *Right:* LaDonna at the keyboard where she still spends many hours each month practicing.

Above:
Herman and
LaDonna
enjoyed a
surprise from
Rex Rudy, who
provided a
carriage for
them to ride off
into the sunset
after their
wedding in Oklahoma City May 3, 1986. *Lower:* In May, 1988, LaDonna's
sister, Ruth Evelyn, left, married Walter Seideman. The ceremony took place in
Herman and LaDonna's backyard.

The Million Dollar Convention

CHAPTER 12

IT WAS THE BIGGEST PROMOTION IN THE
HISTORY OF THE FLORAL INDUSTRY.
HERB MITCHELL

In September, 1984, Herman announced a one
million dollar cash first prize in a three-year AFS promotion that
would surpass any event the floral industry had ever seen. The
promotion, the idea of Herman and AFS director of public
relations Rex Rudy, was unveiled at the Midwest Trade Fair in
Indianapolis, Indiana.

One million dollars in cash, in $100 bills, firmly encased
in one-inch thick unbreakable plexiglass and heavily guarded by
security officers, was on display for the 4,500 florists attending
the trade fair.

"It was one of the most outstanding promotional
ideas I ever heard of," remembered Johnny Childers, "When
someone mentioned the word 'million,' people stopped and

$1,000,000.00

Facing page: The Million Dollar Convention was actually the idea of Rex Rudy, left. He and Herman spent many hours together, working out the details of the successful promotion. *Right:* An advertisement sent to the nation's florists, promoting the Million Dollar Convention and the chance to win a million dollars. Florists received a puzzle piece for every five orders sent through AFS. The puzzle had 300 pieces, but some of the key pieces were made in small quantities, dramatically increasing the odds of only a few florists receiving the right pieces.

This Holiday Season
DOUBLE YOUR CHANCES TO WIN
$1,000,000!

listened. You didn't have to say money, all you had to say was 'million.'"[1]

AFS hired Dan P. Curtin & Associates, a consulting firm that specialized in sweepstakes and contests, to develop and oversee the promotion in which puzzle pieces were sent to florists based upon the number of orders they sent through AFS.

Curtin remembered his first meeting with Herman, "I quickly discovered that Herman was serious about making the transition from AFS being perceived as a discount wire service to a position as tops in the industry."[2]

Herman wanted a highly visible promotion that would cause florists to make a conscious decision to favor AFS when it came time to place a floral order to a retail shop in another town, state, or country. Curtin said, "From the beginning, Herman told me that the prize for the promotion had to be compelling, not just interesting or nice."[3]

Herman also directed Curtin to adopt contest rules that would allow "the small guys" an equal chance to win the million dollars. Eventually, millions of pieces of the jigsaw puzzle were distributed to florists around the world.

Shortly after the Indianapolis convention, every florist in America received rules regarding the Million Dollar Puzzle Sweepstakes. All florists, not just AFS subscribers, were eligible to win the top prize that would be paid at $50,000 a year for 20 years. Because of high interest rates, AFS was able to purchase an annuity from Manufacturers Life Insurance Company for only about $250,000 to cover the cost of the million dollar prize.[4]

During the next three years, the million dollars was displayed at trade fairs and conventions. Most of the time, $100 bills only appeared on the top of stacks of money enclosed in plexiglass. However, at major conventions, AFS would actually wire a million dollars to a local bank and then have security guards accompany the cash for display.

In addition to the top prize, contestants were eligible for thousands of lesser prizes, including television and cutlery sets, video recorders, and microwave ovens. Each month, press packets were released with information about the promotion that would culminate with the winner receiving the top prize at a Million Dollar Convention to be held in August, 1987, in Las Vegas, Nevada.

In July, 1987, just before the Million Dollar Convention, the World Flower Council held a summit meeting and Flower Olympics in Las Vegas. It was the fifth worldwide conference of WFC members whose goal, with Herman as chairman of the organization, was to promote cooperation among florists in more than 150 countries.

There was something for everyone at the Million Dollar Convention at Bally's Hotel in Las Vegas. Special programs were developed for children who accompanied their par-

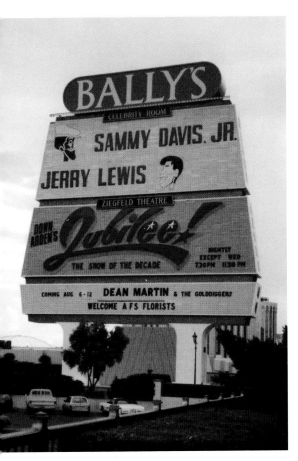

AFS Florists attending the Million Dollar Convention were greeted as they arrived at Bally's Hotel & Casino.

ents. A junior youth program included a visit to the Omnimax Theatre, a hayride, a bowling excursion, and trips to an amusement park and a water park. The senior youth program, for older teenagers, included rafting on the Colorado River.

Herman made it possible for every AFS employee who wanted to, from management to the mailroom, to attend the Million Dollar Convention. "It was a tremendous expense," remembered AFS vice president of finance, Tony Lovio, "but it was worth it. Employees talked about the trip for many years."[5]

Las Vegas Mayor Ron Lurie presented Herman, Tom Butler, and Bob Meinders the keys to the city as he welcomed AFS. The Million Dollar Convention, formally named the Million Dollar Trade Fair, opened to the music of fife and drum as dignitaries cut the ribbon opening the convention.

More than 5,000 florists from thousands of North American towns and cities came to Las Vegas, many hoping to win the million dollars. They had collected puzzle pieces for nearly three years, keeping the AFS name in a prominent position in their lives. Many of them brought the key puzzle pieces with them to the convention.

For entertainment, AFS contracted with singer Toni Tennille, part of the popular Captain and Tennille sensation. However, when Tennille was

Herman, left, and Bob Meinders, help cut the ribbon, officially opening the 1987 AFS Million Dollar Convention in Las Vegas.

unable to perform, comedian and television star Rich Little joined recording artist Mac Davis to provide incredible entertainment.

The main speaker for the convention was Dr. Robert H. Schuller, pastor of the Crystal Cathedral in Garden Grove, California, whose weekly television program, "The Hour of Power," was the most watched religious program in the world. Dr. Schuller, one of the nation's most inspirational speakers, was so popular that florists lined up outside the convention hall where he was speaking hours before the doors were opened.

The final competition for the Great American Design Contest was held during the Million Dollar Convention in the 50,000 square-foot grand ballroom of Bally's Hotel. Winners from ten regional competitions gathered to stretch their creative talents as they reached for the most prestigious design award in the industry. Hitomi Gilliam was named the Gold Medal Winner. Later that year, the American Eagle Award trophy was designed as a permanent tribute to honor the national winners of the Great American Design Contest.

With Rich Little and Mac Davis on stage, Picayune,

Left: **Dr. Robert H. Schuller was the guest motivational speaker at the 1987 Million Dollar Convention.** *Below:* **Herman addresses guests and employees at the Million Dollar Convention at Bally's Hotel in Las Vegas. At Herman's right is AFS president Tom Butler.**

Mississippi, florist Jimmie Jarrell won the million dollars. Her husband, George, had noticed the contest announcement in his mail three years before and had saved several bags of puzzle pieces by the time of the convention. For months, puzzle pieces were stacked on a table in their flower shop workroom and friends would sort through them to find a match.

It was a miracle that the Jarrells were in Las Vegas. They had been in the flower business 22 years but had never taken such a long trip from Mississippi. A friend, a school teacher off

Left: Making certain that the million dollar promotion was operated fairly and legally were, left to right, Dan Curtin, a consultant in such matters, and David Thompson, AFS's auditor in Oklahoma City. *Below*: Jimmie Jarrell, a florist from Mississippi, won the million dollar prize at the 1987 AFS convention. Left to right, Bob Meinders, Tom Butler, and Herman, present a blown-up check for $1 million to Jarrell.

for the summer, volunteered to run the flower shop while Jimmie and George drove to Las Vegas for the AFS convention.[6]

     Jimmie could not believe she won the million dollars. The first thing that came to her mind was the theme of the convention, "It could only happen in America." In fact, she was embarrassed to tell Herman that she and George were not even staying at Bally's for the convention. To cut expenses, they had booked a $50-a-night room at the Half Moon Motel in the valley.

Herman, left, with boyhood friends, Jack Nessen, center, and George Schulze, at the Million Dollar Convention.

However, Herman insisted they stay at Bally's and AFS provided what Jimmie called "the most fabulous room I ever dreamed of seeing."[7]

As soon as Jimmie and George were settled in their room, they called home to talk to a neighbor who was running for

Amy Butler, left, the daughter of AFS president Tom Butler, pauses at the Million Dollar Convention for a photograph with California florist Vic Levy.

a local office in that day's voting. When Jimmie told the neighbor they had won a million dollars, the neighbor thought the Jarrells had gone to Las Vegas and were either drunk or playing a very realistic joke on him.[8]

In 2004, the Jarrells were still receiving a $50,000 check each August and continued to run their flower shop in Mississippi.

Nearly 20 years after the million dollar promotion, Dan Curtin reflected on its success, "It was a one-of-a-kind event in the history of commercial promotion. Everyone at the convention wanted to be there—they thought they could win. There was a high level of energy because some of the people had been

Herman, right, appeared on Capitol Hill in Washington, D.C., as head of the government relations committee of the Society of American Florists. Here, members of the committee talk to United States Senator and, later, Vice President Dan Quayle. Left to right, Ohio floral wholesaler Lindley Mann, Quayle, Washington state grower Paul Shinoda, and Jim Durio, a retail and wholesale florist in Louisiana.

Above: Florists who were top senders of orders through AFS gathered for this photograph in Rio de Janeiro, Brazil. Left to right, Jane Knox, John Byerly, Otto Wentland, Virginia Wentland, Mildred Riddle, Mark Knox, and Sue Byerly. This was the first time in the flowers-by-wire industry that a company thanked its florists by giving them an all-expenses paid trip to a resort. *Right:* In 1990, AFS began accepting orders from florists in the Soviet Union. Anatoli Pitevtsev, left, was the first Soviet florist to visit AFS headquarters in Oklahoma City.

AFS joined the World Flower Council to sponsor an exchange program for floral students. Jim Behrens, AFS's director of education, left, and Herman welcome Japanese students to AFS headquarters in Oklahoma City.

religiously collecting the kooky pieces for three years. The convention had the feel of attending the Oscars."[9]

Florist Review publisher Frances Dudley said about the Million Dollar Convention, "The million dollar giveaway has never been topped. Herman had the ability to create programs and marketing plans unheard of in the industry."[10]

In 1988, the AFS Computer Training Center opened at company headquarters in Oklahoma City. The center, the only one of its kind in the industry, opened for classes in February, 1988.

In April, 1988, the AFS rebate increased again—to $1.50 for orders through 199 and $2.00 per order for florists who had more than 200 orders on the monthly statement. Later that year, Eulalah Overmeyer retired and a bronze sculpture in her likeness was dedicated and placed in the AFS Education Center.

By the end of 1988, AFS had 18,447 florists with an average order value of $29.16. In August, 1989, the first AFS flower order was placed in the Soviet Union and the company was invited to participate the next month in an international design competition in Estonia, one of the Russian republics.

The rebate for orders again was increased in October, 1989, to $3.00 for each order under 200 and $4.00 for each order over 200 each month.

In 1990, legendary broadcaster Paul Harvey was the main speaker for the AFS convention in Orlando, Florida. The

Above: News commentator Paul Harvey was the main speaker at the 1990 AFS convention in Florida. Left to right, Bob Meinders, Marj Meinders, Angel Harvey, Paul Harvey, Cora Diehl, and Cecil Diehl. The Diehls founded National Floral Supply, a chain of about 70 floral shops located on American military bases. *Below:* Among the foreign guests at the AFS convention in Orlando in 1990 were George and Els Hazenberg from The Netherlands. Els was well-known throughout the world as an expert in European floral design.

Left: Christy Meinders, center, with the Smothers Brothers, who provided entertainment at the 1990 AFS convention and trade show in Orlando, Florida.

Right: AFS conventions always had activities planned for children. Marie Ackerman was in charge of kids' programs at the 1990 Orlando convention. *Below:* Jim Morley, left, Eulalah Overmeyer, and Marie Ackerman at the Orlando convention.

Above: Tom Butler, left, and Herman, dressed in bright pink jackets, give an award to Johnny Childers at the Orlando convention.
Left: LaDonna and Herman cut a cake in 1990 celebrating the 20th anniversary of the founding of American Floral Services.

When AFS, with EuroFlorist, bought a wire service in Denmark, the occasion was marked by the participants posing with a copy of the signed agreement. Left to right, Per-Erik Matz, Anders Carlson, Werner Bech, Bodil Bech, Herman, Peter Jungbeck, and Tom Butler.

Smothers Brothers provided comic entertainment for delegates to the convention.

In 1990, the number of AFS subscribers topped the 21,000 mark. The following year, a separate directory was published for AFS Canada. For the first 20 years of the company, Canadian florists were listed in the same directory as United States florists. In 1991, AFS bought Independent Management Systems, Inc. (IMS), a multi-user computer software company headquartered in Birmingham, Michigan.

For the first time ever, AFS launched a national advertising campaign in 1992. Weekly commercials were aired on Paul Harvey News, broadcast to 23 million Americans on 1,300 ABC-affiliated stations.

For the life of the company, directories had been printed at commercial printing companies. However, in 1992, for the first time, directory pages were prepared entirely in-house by computer, eliminating the time consuming manual paste-up before sending them to the printer.

In 1993, AFS joined Oklahoma Olympic gold medalist Shannon Miller to support the National Red Ribbon Celebration, a campaign devoted to promote the benefits of being "drug free and proud" among America's youth.

Selling the Business

CHAPTER 13

FEW MEN HAVE VIRTUE TO WITHSTAND
THE HIGHEST BIDDER.
GEORGE WASHINGTON

By 1993, American Floral Services was closing in on FTD as the leader in the world's flowers-by-wire industry. FTD had 23,738 subscribers, slightly more than 2,000 ahead of AFS at 21,620. Trailing AFS and FTD were Teleflora, 17,255; Redbook, 12,077; Carik, 11,639; and Florafax, 5,926. In the previous two years, AFS was the only wire service to show a net gain in subscribers.[1]

Herman was more involved than ever in civic projects and in promoting the floral industry worldwide. Happy with the job that Tom Butler had done as president of AFS since 1985, Herman began thinking about selling the company.

He was in his mid-fifties and decided to diversify his holdings by liquidating his 100 percent ownership of AFS.

The cover of a special brochure outlining the advantages of joining AFS. The contents of the brochure made up much of the information contained in the offering memorandum prepared for potential buyers.

Herman was growing tired of putting in long days and wanted more personal time with LaDonna and his family. Also, his brother, Bob, was nearly 50 and eager to do something different. To Herman, who had always relied heavily upon Bob to represent his interests in the business, Bob's decision only intensified his resolve to sell AFS.[2]

Herman hired a well-known Irvine, California, investment banking firm, Cruttenden & Company, to assist in selling AFS. Ronald Glickman, Cruttenden's vice president of corporate finance, spent much time in Oklahoma City studying the books and operations of AFS. He prepared an offering memorandum that told the history of the company, its financial performance, and esteemed position in the floral industry. The offering memorandum emphasized that the industry leader, FTD, had proven vulnerable to AFS and that AFS presented a "turnkey" opportunity for a new owner.[3]

AFS had much to offer a potential buyer. The company was serving approximately half of the more than 41,000 retail florists in North America. Business experts agreed that the floral industry was in a rapid and dynamic period of change and would likely increase sales from a record $5.5 billion in 1992. American consumers were annually spending more than $50 per capita on flowers, double the amount they spent a decade before.[4]

An excellent management team was in place at AFS. In addition to Butler, as president, Anthony Lovio was vice president of finance and Mark Nance was vice president of sales.

The coverage of the AFS directory was worldwide, making it easy for florists to send and receive international orders. AFS provided advertising kits, wall calendars, and direct mail brochures to florists. The AFS financial services division offered the Rebate Plus plan, a credit card program that streamlined floral shops' operation, and an audit and recovery program to help florists collect delinquent accounts.[5]

More than 3,000 florists were taking advantage of the AFS Rosebud computer software program to manage their shops. AFS offered the finest educational materials and promotional

Brighten Your Day With Fresh Flowers

It's the special little things that make life worthwhile. Brighten your surroundings and make your day more enjoyable with fresh cut flowers. Flowers add a festive touch to everything—from your dining room table to the desk in your office. And they are so easy and affordable.

Make everyday special with fresh cut flowers. Stop by our shop and we will help you select a bunch of flowers for yourself or a friend.

Make Everyday Special With

fresh flowers

AFS provided small statement stuffers such as this that local florists could use to promote business and the idea of sending flowers on every occasion.

items for florists. AFS published *Professional Floral Designer* and *The Retail Florist,* highly regarded magazines in the industry, and had international distribution rights to *Floral Finance.* AFS also published a series of books, including *Professional Floral Design Manual, The Profit Minded Florist, Tributes, Flowers for Your Wedding,* and *Fundamentals of Profitable Visual Presentations.*

The AFS Education Center was the only permanent center of its kind in the industry. Dedicated to professional floral development, the state-of-the-art facility provided the very latest in floral design, commentating, management, and computer education, taught by experts in the industry. Thousands of florists from around the world came to Oklahoma City to attend sessions at the Education Center. Many more attended AFS Field Education seminars throughout North America.

AFS hosted premier international events; sponsored the Great American Design Contest to showcase design talent; and encouraged careers in the floral industry through a program called "AFS Kids Education."[6]

In addition to its stellar reputation, AFS was a highly profitable operation, with revenue of $36 million and pre-tax income of $9 million in 1992. More than six million orders were processed at a value of more than $200 million. Each of the nearly 22,000 florists paid an initial fee and a $44.95 per month subscriber fee. Many florists also paid from $15 to $35 per month for advertising in the AFS directory. AFS also generated income from sales of magazines, the clearing of credit charges, and from its computer system. By 1993, AFS employed 186 people, including 28 field sales representatives.[7]

As Herman began the transition from sole owner of a huge international company to an individual investor, he looked for someone to manage his business interests. He talked with his brother, Bob, who pointed out that, after a sale, AFS employees no longer could take care of Herman's personal business. After all, people at AFS collected rent on his rental property, kept records on his helicopter, and maintained his house and yard. Bob said, "You really need someone like Mo," referring to Mo Grotjohn, president of Jefferson Bank & Trust in Denver, Colorado.

Herman had become a stockholder and director of the bank because of his close relationship with Ben Veldkamp, one of Denver's largest florists. Eventually, Herman became the largest stockholder and worked closely with Grotjohn. They became friends, partly because of their similar backgrounds. Grotjohn was born in a small town, Schaller, Iowa, and grew up on a farm. He was a CPA with a national accounting firm before getting into the banking business.[8]

Grotjohn, who knew that Herman was thinking of selling AFS, received a call from Herman early in the morning on October 18, 1993. Herman told Grotjohn about his conversation with Bob and said, "Would you be interested in moving here and helping me out?" Grotjohn said, "Yes," and assured Herman that maybe he could come to Oklahoma City the following week to talk about it.[9]

However, Herman was in his usual hurry. He told Grotjohn that he had received several offers to purchase the company and needed to make some decisions. Herman said, "Why don't you catch a plane today?" Grotjohn agreed and made immediate plans to fly to Oklahoma City that afternoon. After talking with Herman and LaDonna, he was hired.

Grotjohn really did not have to think long and hard about coming to work for Herman on such short notice. He had grown to respect Herman greatly and knew Herman's word was his bond. Grotjohn remembered, "I had been impressed with his complete integrity, candor, decency, honesty, and his steel-trap memory. Years after he stopped traveling the country, if you named a town in the United States, he could tell you the name of the florists there."[10]

Grotjohn's employment was timely because he was allowed to play an active role in discussing each of four purchase offers and to advise Herman on taxable consequences of sale terms. Herman, Bob Meinders, Grotjohn, investment banker Ronald Glickman, Chicago, Illinois attorney Mike Sklar, and AFS auditor David Thompson spent many hours reviewing the purchase offers. Herman, still concerned about his employees at

Herman, front left, hands an AFS key to Tom Butler, signifying his trust in the AFS management team.

Herman and his secretary of 25 years, Evelyn Chappell, left. On the day she interviewed for the job, her future office was tidy and orderly. However, when she arrived on her first day, stacks of work were piled everywhere. Evelyn enjoyed the family atmosphere at AFS and welcomed Herman's daughter, Christy, on visits to the office. Before Christy started school, she often spent a couple of afternoons a week at the office, along with her toys, books, and videotapes. Of Herman, Evelyn says, "He is still absolutely impossible to predict!"

AFS, rejected the highest offer because it was obvious that the group would replace many members of AFS top management and move the company headquarters from Oklahoma City.

Herman decided to pursue the sale of AFS to Chemical Venture Partners (CVP), an investment arm of Chemical Bank, based in New York City. He called Steve Murray, a CVP principal and said, "There are some things in your offer that we need to change, but I think we can make a deal."[11]

The following day, Murray flew to Oklahoma City and began meeting with Herman, Bob, Grotjohn, Glickman, and Sklar. Herman had three conditions which he insisted be part of any agreement to sell AFS—the company headquarters must stay in Oklahoma City, management and employees must remain in place, and the generous employee profit-sharing plan had to continue for at least two years.[12]

The match with CVP showed great potential because Herman was looking for a buyer who would leave things in place.

Grotjohn remembered, "Chemical, because of its nature, was content to purchase a company and let existing management run it. Other bidders wanted to actually run the company and control where the headquarters was."[13]

The huge deal was struck just two days after Herman decided to pursue an agreement with CVP. After Herman was satisfied with preliminary sale terms including cash and notes, a letter of intent was signed.

Lawyers and accountants worked four months on stacks of documents necessary to complete the sale of the company that was founded in a garage apartment just 24 years before. Closing on the sale was set for February 18, 1994.

Two weeks before the sale, Herman, LaDonna, and Grotjohn were in New York City working out last minute details of the complicated agreement. During a Sunday afternoon meeting with Glickman, Sklar, and Grotjohn, CVP's Murray attempted to change some of the terms of the agreement. Grotjohn told Murray, "You don't want to do this. Herman doesn't have to sell the company. He will walk away and go back to Oklahoma City in a minute."[14]

Herman had prearranged plans to dine with Murray that evening at one of Manhattan's famous restaurants. However, after Grotjohn, Glickman, and Sklar told Herman about the changes during a brief conference in the bar at the Waldorf-Astoria Hotel, Herman said, "Well, I'm not having dinner with the guy. We'll just go home tomorrow."[15]

Attorney Sklar excused himself, saying he was going to the restroom. However, Sklar called Murray and alerted him to the fact that Herman was upset. Thirty minutes later, Murray walked into the bar and tried to explain away last minute changes with the comment, "That's just the way it is in deals like this." An obviously irritated Herman replied, "No, Steve, that's not how these things work. We have been working for three months and have everything in writing."

Herman continued, "Steve, what you don't understand is that I don't have to sell the company. I'm only 56 years old and the company is doing great. It's not like you have me over a barrel." The next day, after another meeting, Murray withdrew

Above: Herman and daughter, Christine, on the day she graduated from George Washington University in May, 2000. Christine, known in her younger years as Christy, now works in New York City. *Right:* Herman and LaDonna at the Fortune Club Christmas party in 1998.

The Fortune Club
Christmas 1998

his planned changes and the deal proceeded.[16]

There was one last hurdle to clear. Just before closing at the law offices of Simpson, Thatcher, and Bartlett in Manhattan, Murray told Herman that one of the investors in the CVP group, 1-800-Flowers (800 Flowers), a company that had carved for itself a good sized share of the market of floral orders with its toll-free number, wanted a better investment deal than had originally been planned. When Herman said, "No," Murray told his attorney, "Kill the deal."[17]

Grotjohn told CVP attorneys, "Herman will take care of this." And Herman did. He called 800 Flowers owner Jim McCann, who agreed to keep the deal the same. With all matters resolved, Herman signed a mountain of papers and ownership of AFS transferred to CVP.[18]

CVP offered Herman the opportunity to continue to office at AFS headquarters, but Herman declined, thinking his presence on the property might give mixed signals to employees. With his longtime secretary, Evelyn Chappell, and Grotjohn, Herman moved into offices in the Union Bank Building on the Northwest Expressway in Oklahoma City. The office was later moved to Perimeter Center near Herman and LaDonna's home on Lombardy Lane in northwest Oklahoma City.[19]

In 2000, AFS merged with Teleflora, owned by entrepreneur Stewart Resnick. Resnick operated thousands of acres of agricultural properties in California and owned the Franklin Mint.

Herman agreed the new combined companies would operate under the name Teleflora, as he understood the influence the name had in overseas markets. He readily endorsed the merger and name change.

Herman and Resnick had been strong competitors. Gregg Coccari, the president of Teleflora, remembered the interesting dinner at which Herman and Resnick discussed their old times of competing, "In a friendly way, they were arguing about whom cost who the most money."[20]

Tom Butler was made chairman and Coccari was named president and chief executive officer of Teleflora with offices in Oklahoma City; Los Angeles, California; Paragould,

Herman rests momentarily from the laborious task of signing his name hundreds of times on documents relating to the sale of AFS. He was proud of his accomplishments at AFS. Once during an interview in his office, a reporter observed the many expensive and rare mementos of Herman's travels, and asked, "What's the most important item in this office?" Herman quickly pointed to his first AFS directory, and said, "That little red book over there!"

Arkansas; O'Fallon, Missouri; and Toronto, Canada. To remain competitive in the new century, Teleflora used cutting edge technology to lead the industry in Internet marketing and provide an electronic network to make it cost-effective for florists to send and receive orders.

Herman was given the title of chairman emeritus of the new company that dominated the flowers-by-wire portion of an industry that had grown to $15 billion annually.

Herman never looked back. He was proud of the company he founded in the North Classen garage apartment...but he gladly looked forward to spending time developing a comprehensive plan to share his wealth with others.

Above: Herman, right, at the closing of his sale of AFS to Chemical Venture Partners. Left to right, Tom Butler, Steve Murray of CVP, and Ron Glickman, the consultant who brokered the sale.

Right: A portion of one of the many rows of documents to be signed to consummate the sale of AFS in 1994. This is one of three rooms which contained tables filled with documents. Two of the rooms at the New York City law firm used in the closing were where scenes from the movie, "Bonfire of the Vanities," starring Tom Hanks and Melanie Griffith, actually took place.

Top: Celebrating the merger of AFS and Teleflora in November, 2000, were, left to right, Stewart Resnick, owner of Teleflora; Teleflora president Gregg Coccari, Tom Butler, and Herman. *Above:* Teleflora senior vice president of sales Jack Howard, Teleflora president and chief executive officer Phil Kleweno, and Teleflora Chairman Tom Butler. *Courtesy Teleflora.*

Hundreds gathered on January 27, 2004, to dedicate the Meinders School of Business. Note the large "M" and logo of the business school on the floor of the rotunda of the three-story building. Herman was proud of his association with OCU, and the university felt the same. OCU honored Herman with its Distinguished Alumnus Award in 1985 and an Honorary Doctor of Commercial Science degree in 1989. *Courtesy Oklahoma City University.*

A Charitable Heart

CHAPTER 14

HERMAN WAS USUALLY GOOD WITH NUMBERS-
BUT FOR SOME REASON, HE BELIEVED
'TITHING' MEANT GIVING 50 PERCENT.
MO GROTJOHN

GENUINE GENEROSITY IS NOT ARROGANT,
OBVIOUS, OR EXCHANGED.
MARTY GRUBBS, CROSSINGS COMMUNITY CHURCH

From his childhood at St. Paul Lutheran Church in Pipestone, Herman was taught the value of giving to his church and to charitable projects. During his years of driving thousands of miles each month, he became a regular listener of "The Lutheran Hour," the radio program of the Lutheran Church-Missouri Synod. He took to heart sermons he heard about being a good citizen and sharing one's good fortune with others from the radio program and from "This is the Life," the Lutheran sponsored television program.

The tenor of Herman's desire to give back to the community in which he enjoyed incredible business success may

Left: The Kramer School of Nursing on the Oklahoma City University campus is a 16,500-square-foot state-of-the-art facility that features television monitoring to each classroom to allow demonstrations from a central laboratory, and teaching at various levels to each classroom. Herman, LaDonna, and the Kramer family appeared at the November 23, 1994, dedication of the building. Left to right, Ruth Evelyn Kramer Seideman, E.J. Kramer, Alma Kramer, Herman, and LaDonna. *Lower left:* When Herman sold AFS in 1994, he was able to devote much of his time to civic and charitable projects. He also served as a trustee of Oklahoma City University and a trustee of the American Floral Endowment and the World Flower Council.

have been revealed most clearly in the first few months in which Mo Grotjohn handled Herman's business affairs.

In a December, 1993, meeting shortly before Herman sold AFS to Chemical Venture Partners, Herman asked Grotjohn how much in contributions he could deduct. When Grotjohn advised him that he could deduct up to 50 percent of his adjusted gross income, and that he could contribute an additional $2 million that year, Herman said, "Well, let's figure out who we're going to give that $2 million to."[1]

Grotjohn quickly followed Herman's direction and made arrangements to give the $2 million to worthy causes identified by Herman and LaDonna.[2]

Giving was not a new idea for Herman. Since his teenage years working at the J. C. Penney store in his hometown, Herman had regularly supported his church and willingly gave of his money and time to civic projects. He was aware of C.S. Lewis's comment that "good and evil both increase at compound interest." Herman wanted to make certain that he spread good as far as possible with everyone he met and every group with which he had contact.

As he became financially sound in the 1980s at AFS, he intentionally looked for causes and organizations to which he could contribute and lend support. He regarded his employees as

Herman and LaDonna read the plaque that commemorates their contribution for the construction of the Meinders Foyer in the Gonda Building at the Mayo Clinic in Rochester, Minnesota. On the trip to dedicate the foyer in September, 2002, LaDonna noticed swelling in one of her legs. Herman said, "Let's get it checked out while we're here." Doctors found an enlarged lymph node and removed the cancerous tissue in surgery.

one of the biggest factors of the company's success and wanted to be generous in AFS's participation in employee benefit programs.

Above: In 1998, Herman received Oklahoma's highest honor when he was inducted into the Oklahoma Hall of Fame, sponsored by the Oklahoma Heritage Association. The 1998 Hall of Fame class was prestigious. Left to right, Dr. Donald Cooper, fitness expert; Dr. W. French Anderson, the father of human gene therapy; Wanda L. Bass, banker and philanthropist; Reba McEntire, recording artist and actress; Herman; and businessman Archie Dunham. *Right:* Herman was presented for induction by Dr. Robert H. Schuller, left. Here Schuller congratulates Herman and superstar Reba McEntire on their achievement.

Herman had always harbored fond memories of his year at Oklahoma City University and was quick to respond to requests for help from the university. In the 1980s, he contributed substantial funds to establish scholarships and a chair at the OCU business school. In turn, OCU named the school the Meinders School of Business. In the 1990s, more than 6,500 Master of Business Administration students graduated from the school that was located on campus in the Noble Center for Competitive Enterprise.

Habitat for Humanity was a good example of a charity which caught Herman's attention. The Central Oklahoma Habitat for Humanity chapter constructed dozens of homes for less fortunate families. Herman said, "I will never forget going to homes where people lived in a quality house for maybe the first time in their lives. Seeing the results of our donations was a special reward."[3]

Dozens of other projects were supported by Herman and LaDonna. With the help of Leamon Freeman, Herman's friend who was a district judge in Oklahoma County, and Donna Corjay, A Better Choice (ABC), which helped disadvantaged youth learn literacy skills to be able to better compete in the business world, was founded.

Ray Ackerman, founder of the state's largest advertising agency and longtime civic leader, said, "From preserving history to the United Way, Herman was always generous." During one United Way fund-raising campaign, Ackerman went to Herman's office to ask for a contribution from AFS. Herman pulled out his personal checkbook and wrote United Way a $50,000 check.[4]

Herman strongly supported Lambda Chi Alpha, the fraternity of which he was an active member in his one year of attendance at OCU. Businessman Vince Orza, a fraternity brother and fellow trustee of OCU and other organizations, has worked with Herman in many civic projects. Orza said, "Herman's story is one that everyone ought to hear. He doesn't wag his finger and tell you how hard he has worked—but instead, when he has made a personal commitment to a project, he quietly says, 'I'd

Left: Herman receiving an award from the Wholesale Florists and Floral Suppliers of America. For his contributions to the floral industry, Herman received the highest awards of many organizations. He was elected to the American Academy of Florists, given an honorary membership in the American Institute of Floral Designers, received the AIFD Award of Merit, and for many years was chairman of the World Flower Council. *Below:* Flanked by members of Lambda Chi Alpha, Herman Meinders receives a Lifetime Achievement Award from fraternity brother Vince Orza, center.

like you to help me do some of these things.'"[5]

Lambda Chi awarded Herman the Order of Achievement and Order of Merit, the fraternity's highest honors. Ironically, the only other person ever to receive both awards was the late Alfred P. Murrah, a federal appeals court judge who also lived in Oklahoma City.

Former Oklahoma City mayor and fellow OCU trustee, Ron Norick, remembered Herman's anonymous contributions to OCU over the years. Many times, Herman quietly gave money to OCU to acquire residential property adjacent to the campus so the university could expand its physical plant. Norick said, "Often, President Jerald Walker would announce at a trustees meeting that an anonymous donor had provided funds to acquire six or eight more houses—but we all knew it was Herman. He was embarrassed if we said anything about it."[6]

Herman's sister, Linda Rice, observed, "Oklahoma gave Herman such a good life and a great opportunity to succeed, he wanted to give back to the state and its people. His desire for education is overwhelming."[7]

In August, 1994, Herman and LaDonna retired the remaining debt on a new nursing school building at OCU. The school was then named the Kramer School of Nursing in honor of LaDonna's parents, E.J. and Alma Kramer. The new building housed three classrooms, the Student Health Center, a simulated hospital skills lab, and a computer and audio visual learning lab.

In addition to giving back to his community and state, Herman gave enormous time and assets to the floral industry. Floral products magnate Pete

Express Personnel Services founder Bob Funk, right, congratulates Herman in 1992 on his induction into the Sales and Marketing Executives Academy of Achievement.

Herman joined a prestigious class of inductees of the Sales and Marketing Executives Academy of Achievement in 1992. Left to right, sitting, Herb Kelleher, founder of Southwest Airlines; Herman; and Carl Pohlad, owner of the Minnesota Twins and Minnesota Vikings. Standing, Scott De Garmo, publisher of *Success* magazine; Rocky Aoki, founder of the Benihana of Tokyo restaurant chain; S. Truett Cathy, founder of Chik-Fil-A; Ken Evans, accepting for Dean Buntrock, co-founder of Waste Management, Inc.; and Perry Rogers, accepting for the late Joyce Hall, founder of Hallmark. *Courtesy Oklahoma Publishing Company.*

Garcia said, "Herman saw our industry as more than a business—he was interested in our personal lives, our successes, and our disappointments. Many people give their money to causes, but Herman gave his heart to his thousands of florist friends around the world."[8]

Even though he was no longer active in running the major flowers-by-wire service in the country, Herman continued to participate actively in industry organizations such as the American Floral Endowment (AFE), a group founded in 1961 by John Henry Dudley and Charles Pennock to fund programs to help improve the floralculture industry. AFE funds scientific research at colleges and universities and supports educational programs that

benefit the industry.

Steve Martinez, executive vice president of AFE, liked board members like Herman. He said, "Some people just serve on boards to be serving. However, Herman really believed in the endowment and in our mission—when a project needed to be completed, he was the first one to say, 'I'll do it!'"[9]

Shortly before selling AFS, Herman and LaDonna founded The Meinders Foundation, which contributed, in its first ten years, nearly $12 million to 124 projects in 16 states and 12 cities in Oklahoma. The first project was a $50,000 contribution to the Omniplex, a unique learning center and museum in Oklahoma City, founded by Admiral John Kirkpatrick.[10]

Among the major projects and organizations funded by The Meinders Foundation are Allied Arts, Calm Waters, Community Literacy Centers, the Education and Employment Ministry, Great Expectations Foundation, Junior Achievement of Greater Oklahoma City, Oklahoma City Philharmonic, Oklahoma City Museum of Art, Special Care, Red Cross, Salvation Army, and the Oklahoma Council of Public Affairs.[11]

Herman's heart for education is clear when one reads the list of dozens of educational institutions supported by Herman personally and The Meinders Foundation. Major gifts have been made to Oklahoma City University, Concordia University in Selma, Alabama, Concordia University in Seward, Nebraska, Concordia Seminary in St. Louis, Missouri, the Oklahoma School of Science and Mathematics, Northeastern State University, the Oklahoma Educational Television Authority, Oklahoma Christian University, Oklahoma State University, University of Oklahoma, Patrick Henry College, Southern Nazarene University, St. Gregory's College, the University of Central Oklahoma, and many other institutions of higher learning and education-focused organizations.[12]

The Foundation made major contributions to the Oklahoma

Heritage Association; Phillips Theological Seminary in Tulsa, Oklahoma, for the construction of the Meinders Chapel; the Myriad Gardens Foundation, for development of the Meinders Gardens; the Mayo Clinic, for construction of the Meinders Foyer; the Oklahoma Historical Society; Oklahoma City YMCA; City Rescue Mission; the Lutheran Church-Missouri Synod; Central Oklahoma Habitat for Humanity; Oklahoma Centennial 2007; and Herman's hometown school district in Pipestone, Minnesota.[13]

The contribution to the hometown school came after friend George Schulze informed Herman that Pipestone residents had three times rejected a bond issue to replace the 80-year-old school building where he and Herman had attended classes. Schulze was looking for new ways to entice conservative farmers in the area to support the construction of a new school—so he called Herman.

Herman promised to give the school district $1 million to build a library—if voters would approve a bond issue to construct a new high school building. Schulze broke out in tears when he announced Herman's offer to the Pipestone school board.[14]

Within months, motivated by Herman's generosity, Pipestone voters overwhelmingly approved a bond issue to build a new $23 million high school and education complex. The library is named the Meinders Community Library.[15]

Herman also contributed his parents' farm property to his boyhood church, St. Paul Lutheran. Part of the funds received from the sale of the property was used to purchase a new organ for the church.[16]

In addition to projects funded by The Meinders Foundation, Herman and LaDonna contributed to organizations and projects in the 1990s and early part of the 21st century. Herman was not enthusiastic about the need for a dome for the Oklahoma State Capitol. But one day while he was at his ranch, Herman received a call from Oklahoma Governor Frank Keating, explaining why Oklahoma needed the dome to improve its image. Governor Keating was persuasive, and Herman agreed to

At the dedication of the new dome on the Oklahoma State Capitol are, left to right, Ryan Wuerch, Miss America Shawntel Smith Wuerch, LaDonna and Herman, First Lady Cathy Keating, Governor Frank Keating, Nedra and Bob Funk.

give $1 million toward construction of the dome. Herman and LaDonna's names are emblazoned along with other donors in the Capitol Rotunda as a testament to future generations of their generosity. Also, the Meinders Hall of Mirrors was the result of contributions made during Oklahoma City's renovation of the Civic Center.

In 1999, Herman was approached by OCU President Steve Jennings about making a contribution to repair the building in which the Meinders School of Business was located. However, after repair estimates were received, it was decided that a better course of action was to build a new building for the business school. Herman promised to give $3 million of a projected total cost of $9 million if OCU could commit $3 million of its own and raise $3 million more, which Herman promised to help raise.[17]

The project to build a new business school never got off the ground until Tom McDaniel became president of OCU.

After McDaniel took office at OCU, Herman told him of his offer to fund one-third of the cost of construction of a new business school.

The character of the project changed dramatically on February 12, 2002, when Herman told Mo Grotjohn, "I didn't sleep very well last night. The school deal is really bothering me. I really want to get it done. I am confident with Tom McDaniel as president, this is the time to do it—so I've decided to just do it myself and not have to worry about raising the rest of the money."[18]

The following morning, Herman and Grotjohn met President McDaniel for breakfast at the Classen Grill, a famous breakfast café

Above: **By April 9, 2003, the steel framework of the new Meinders School of Business at Oklahoma City University was in place.** *Courtesy Manhattan Construction Company.* **Right: A crane places the clock on the tower of the new business school during final weeks of construction in 2003.** *Courtesy Manhattan Construction Company.*

Left: Herman, left, OCU President Tom McDaniel, LaDonna, and Meinders School of Business Dean Bart Ward don hard hats to look at progress on the new business school building. *Courtesy Manhattan Construction Company.*

Right: Herman, left, and Mo Grotjohn examine the final beam to be placed at topping-out ceremonies for the new building. *Courtesy Manhattan Construction Company.*

Left: Herman's daughters, Christy, left, and Kathy, inspect the Meinders School of Business during construction. *Courtesy Manhattan Construction Company.*

stuck in an old building in north Oklahoma City. Herman announced his intention to completely fund the business school, at a new projected cost of $13 million. McDaniel, stunned, but immensely thankful, said, "What do we need to do?"[19]

Herman told McDaniel that after he had made that decision, he slept very well for the remainder of the night. Grotjohn said, "Herman may have slept good, but when he told me we needed $13 million for the building, I didn't sleep well— we would have to do some major money juggling."[20]

Herman's brother, Bob, contributed funds for the construction of a plaza on the east side of the Meinders School of Business. Here, Bob is joined by his sister, Linda Rice.

Herman addresses guests during the dedication of the business school building in January, 2004. The Meinders School of Business features state-of-the-art technology that is unsurpassed at other business schools. *Courtesy Oklahoma City University.*

After preliminary agreements were executed, Herman, Grotjohn, and Manhattan Construction Company officials began work on obtaining bids on the project that ultimately cost $18.5 million, all funded by Herman. During construction, Herman and Grotjohn were on the job most days, working

Above: Helping celebrate the dedication of the new Meinders School of Business were, standing, left to right, Norman Cobb, who leases Herman's eastern Oklahoma ranch, Ashley Bowen, Kyle Murphy, and William Alvarez. Seated, Patricia Stratton, Sarah McClain, Stone Sanders, and Melissa Harris. *Below:* LaDonna, left, Herman, and Oklahoma Governor Brad Henry listen to other speakers during the dedication of the Meinders School of Business in 2004. *Courtesy Oklahoma City University.*

The completed project—the Meinders School of Business on the Oklahoma City University campus in Oklahoma City. The building was built on an entire two-square-block area formerly occupied by small houses. It was in this area that Herman lived in an apartment when he first arrived in Oklahoma City more than four decades earlier.

closely with building superintendents and subcontractors to assure that the new Meinders School of Business would be the finest building of its kind at any university.

Oklahoma Governor Brad Henry joined hundreds of public officials, civic and business leaders, and students to dedicate the new business school on January 27, 2004. The state-of-the art facility bore both Herman's name and his inspiration.

Herman's service to Oklahoma City University was praised by Methodist Bishop Bruce Blake, "Herman is a purpose-driven man. Whatever the project is, whatever the purposes of the institution happen to be, he is just driven by that purpose."

Home on the Range: The Diamond "H" Ranch

CHAPTER 15

A HUNTING TRIP ON HERMAN'S RANCH IS
LIKE GOING HUNTING AT THE RAMADA.
TONY LOVIO

After years of long workdays, Herman looked forward to spending more leisure and family time, especially on his 6,000-acre ranch in northeast Oklahoma. He loved the outdoors and had often hunted in Texas, but wanted his own land in Oklahoma. In 1984, he began purchasing parcels of land that were combined into the Diamond "H" Ranch, nestled in the Cookson Hills in Cherokee and Sequoyah counties. The nearest town is Cookson, named for John H. Cookson, the town's first postmaster, in 1895.

The area is rich in history. After the Cherokees were

Top: Herman points to a map of the ranch in the bunkhouse. The ranch lies in two counties in eastern Oklahoma. *Left:* The preferred mode of transportation on the Diamond "H" Ranch is a four-wheeler. In this photograph, Herman directs visitors around the ranch.

driven from their lands in the southeastern United States, they arrived at their new home in Indian Territory via the Trail of Tears. Near the Diamond "H" Ranch is Park Hill, where early missionary Samuel A. Worcester brought Christianity to the Cherokees. A printing press at Park Hill printed more than 25 million pages of materials in Cherokee and English during 25 years in the middle of the 19th century. Until after the Civil War, Park Hill was the center of culture and learning in the Cherokee Nation.[1]

On the original ranch purchased by Herman were a

Right: The official brand of the ranch is the Diamond "H." *Below:* Jeanne St. Cyr managed the Diamond "H" Ranch for many years. She lived next door to the original American Floral Services office in Oklahoma City and, at age 18, began babysitting for Herman's daughter, Kathy. Since that time, St. Cyr has often worked for Herman's enterprises.

small house and several barns. In 1989, Herman and LaDonna built an 8,000-square-foot ranch house that had plenty of space for entertaining friends and customers.

The house, located three and a half miles from a paved road, and at the end of a rocky, gravel road, is a beautiful combination of stone and wood, built on a cliff overlooking a waterfall on glistening Terrapin Creek that flows through the ranch. The multi-level structure has two huge bunk rooms where dozens of guests can sleep and a loft for grandchildren. In Herman's office hangs a sign, "This is my ranch and I'll do as I please."

In the dining room is a magnificent sculpture, by Oklahoman Harold T. Holden, of a cowboy roping a calf to be branded. When Herman saw a model of the work, he noticed it had a different brand from his own. On the copy of the sculpture that Herman and LaDonna bought from Holden, the Diamond "H" brand appears on the hip of the cow and on the branding irons.[2]

For many years, the Diamond "H" was a working ranch—raising cattle, buffalo, llamas, and mustang ponies. However, because of his childhood memories, there were no chickens, pigs, or milk cows on the property. It was common for Herman to arise before daybreak to prepare for branding cows with a Diamond "H" branding iron he had fashioned. Later, he used a more efficient, electric branding iron.[3]

When Herman was still active in managing AFS, he used the ranch to entertain customers and friends. During deer hunting season, many hunters flocked to the ranch to be hosted

Above: Herman at one of the many hunting blinds located on the Diamond "H" Ranch. *Left:* Several of the ponds and lakes on the ranch are named for Herman and LaDonna's grandchildren. Mable is Herman's pet name for his granddaughter, Valerie Gooden.

Above: Lily pads cover the end of one of the 55 lakes and ponds on the Diamond "H" Ranch. *Right:* Herman and co-author, Bob Burke, left, at the entrance to the three-room natural cave on the ranch. A waterfall rushes from the rocks above to a creek below the entrance.

in fine fashion. AFS executive Tony Lovio said, "It was not like sleeping in a tent—we were in a bunkhouse, warm and comfortable."[4]

Hunters were gently awakened at 5:00 a.m. and driven to a modern blind in the middle of the area where deer roamed. Lovio described a typical blind, "It had plexiglass windows and was like a house on stilts. Some people had CD players and a stash of snacks. If you happened to see a deer come by, hey, pull up your gun and shoot." Following the morning hunt, they were fed a hearty breakfast prepared by Herman's brother-in-law, Walter Seideman, and Larry Hendershott.[5]

Hunters were expected to stay in their blinds and know the difference between a deer and a cow. Herman kiddingly told his friends that if they killed one of his cows, it would cost them $1,000. When a hunter killed a deer, Herman's ranch hands dressed and prepared the animal for freezing.[6]

"Hunting with Herman was an unforgettable experience," remembered Pennsylvania florist Scott Edwards, who joined dozens of florists from several states on a typical hunting expedition to the ranch during Thanksgiving season. Edwards had never shot a deer when he made his first hunting trip to the ranch. On the first morning, Herman handed Edwards the gun he had used to shoot his first deer. Ironically, Edwards bagged his first deer that day.[7]

Many visitors to the Diamond "H" simply enjoyed the ranching atmosphere. Tupelo, Mississippi wholesale florist Peggy Bishop loved sending her husband, Harold, and their sons to the ranch to mend fences, knock out beaver dams, and feed the animals. She said, "They could not wait to get to the ranch. My boys think Mr. Herman is the finest man there ever was."[8]

Guest florists at the ranch never felt any pressure from Herman to send more orders through AFS. Ken Freytag from Austin, Texas, was invited to the ranch even though his allegiance in the 1980s was to FTD. He remembered, "Often, when you are invited to someone's house, there are strings attached—but not Herman's ranch. I was a guest and Herman never once asked me for my business."[9] But, because of the friendship with Herman, when FTD became "just another company owned by someone else," Freytag switched his entire wire service business to AFS.[10]

The ranch was much more than just a place to entertain—it was a refuge for Herman and LaDonna from their busy days in the city. Jim Morley observed, "The ranch brought a calm to Herman that I had not seen before. He was anxious to leave his office and get to the ranch when he could. He would

Right: Herman enjoys showing the ranch to visitors. It takes a full day by four-wheeler to adequately investigate the varied parts of the Diamond "H." *Center:* Mo Grotjohn, left, and Herman, in front of Herman's French-made Air Speciale M-350 helicopter which made trips to the ranch in northeast Oklahoma quicker. With good winds, it took less than an hour to fly to the ranch from the helipad at Baptist Hospital in Oklahoma City. Herman became a proficient helicopter pilot, but always flew with pilot Jim Johnson. Herman had two close calls—in low visibility, he once barely missed a television tower. *Below:* The original home on the Diamond "H" Ranch when Herman purchased it in 1984 was small and insufficient to host friends and customers of AFS.

Left: The entrance to the modern ranch home built by Herman and LaDonna in 1989 is guarded by a huge oak tree. *Center:* The game room of the ranch house is a spacious room that allows guests to play pool, video games, or just sit and talk. *Below:* The south deck of the ranch house allows visitors to relax and enjoy the closeness of nature.

rather be brush hogging than looking at financial statements."[11]

Dean White said, "Building a retreat for himself at the ranch balanced and rounded-out Herman's personality. The combination of marrying LaDonna and developing the ranch gave him peace and much personal satisfaction."[12]

The ranch was very special to Herman's family. His and LaDonna's children and grandchildren looked forward to spending holidays and summer vacations at the ranch. The Diamond "H" played an important role in Herman becoming close to LaDonna's parents. Mr. Kramer's only hobby was

Members of the Lambda Chi Alpha chapter at Oklahoma City University worked on the ranch as a fundraiser. Fraternity members picked up rocks and painted fences, while having the time of their lives.

gunsmithing and he enjoyed talking to Herman about hunting and guns. Mrs. Kramer loved going to the ranch in Herman's helicopter—sparing the long drive in a car.[13]

Herman made the Kramers feel like celebrities. He named one of the hunting blinds the Kramer Blind—a move that endeared him to his father-in-law. Herman and LaDonna spent many evenings playing moon, a domino game, with her parents.[14]

Anyone who visits the ranch immediately recognizes Herman's great respect for the land. Since he began acquiring the property, he has labored alongside paid help and volunteers to remove rocks and stumps to produce gently rolling pastures knee deep in native grasses and clover. Among the thickets and

Former Oklahoma Governor David Hall feeding a llama named Alice at the Diamond "H" in 1987.

Herman hosted many friends at the ranch. Left to right, Herman, Bill Williams, and Fred Swindle all formerly worked together at National Florist Directory.

canyons, and around the 55 ponds and two large lakes, live dozens of species of wild birds and animals.

Some of the ponds are named for the Meinders grandchildren, and one large lake is called Lake LaDonna. When the lake was being improved, as many as five beavers a day were taken from the water, to prevent them from building and rebuilding dams.[15]

Herman has worked hard to live up to his own rule that one should leave land in better shape than when it is

Herman won his mother-in-law's heart in 1987 when he used the helicopter to fly her to granddaughter Lori's wedding in Austin, Texas. Alma Kramer was afraid to fly a commercial airliner to Texas, but consented to Herman flying her in the helicopter. Lori was shocked when her grandmother arrived in presidential style in the helicopter. Here, Herman kisses Mrs. Kramer as her husband, E.J. Kramer, waits to board the aircraft.

Left: Herman and a group of Lambda Chi members from Oklahoma City University at the ranch. Left to right, grandson, Stark Kremeier, Ty Weaver, Kyle Evans, Tommy Neathery, and Herman.

Right: Florists Ben VeldKamp, left, and Paul Wentland, center, with Herman on an early hunting trip at the ranch. In this photograph, they are standing in front of the old ranch house.

Left: Mustang horses are bred and raised on the Diamond "H" Ranch.

Right: This longhorn was a birthday gift from LaDonna to Herman.

Herman's nephew, Andrew Rice, shows off his catch from one of the Diamond "H" lakes.

purchased. He joined forces with the Oklahoma Department of Wildlife Conservation to improve the deer population on the ranch and has set aside 600 acres of the ranch as a protected wildlife reserve. Huge expenditures have been made to improve drainage on roads and prevent erosion of topsoil.

Visitors traverse the expansive ranch primarily on four-wheelers on a primitive gravel road that once served as the primary route between Tahlequah and Marble City. Hidden in one draw adjacent to the road is a three-room natural cave, carved into the limestone by thousands of years of flowing water. Before

ABC News commentator Paul Harvey visited the Diamond "H" Ranch during the years when American Floral Services was a sponsor of Harvey's daily broadcasts. In this photograph, Harvey is surely telling a friendly llama "the rest of the story." Harvey, one of the nation's most popular veteran newscasters, grew up in nearby Tulsa, Oklahoma.

Left: The bunkhouse at the Diamond "H" Ranch is equipped to feed dozens of hungry hunters and guests. *Below:* Jamie Fang, left, who served as Herman's interpreter on trips to the Far East, visited the ranch and helped Herman feed buffalo.

Herman bought the ranch, an attorney made his reclusive home in the cave and equipped it with running water and a propane refrigerator. The cave is heated by a fireplace and has a large opening for a window at its entrance that is covered by a cascade of water falling 30 feet into the creek below. In earlier days, the cave was a haven for outlaws in eastern Oklahoma. There exists one legend that famed outlaw, Charles "Pretty Boy" Floyd, who grew up in Sequoyah County, occasionally hid from the law in the cave.[16]

In 1993, news commentator Paul Harvey visited the ranch and featured it in a national radio broadcast. Harvey said, "In Herman Meinders' helicopter, I went into the storied Cookson Hills in autumn, the splendor displayed like a peacock luring us across Tenkiller Lake…Wild deer and wild turkey share the wide

backyard of his home. Tame llamas stroll the barn lot, enormous buffalo share pastures with longhorn steers."[17]

Harvey described the limestone cave he saw, "Just downhill from Red Spring, on the old Marble City Road, a foot off the roadside, into a deep ravine and back up underneath the road, I explored the still-intact, three-room hide-a-way cave where the aristocracy of early outlaws tethered their horses and made themselves at home—while pursuers likely passed at a gallop not ten feet over their heads. With spring waters, laired rabbits, and tin cup whiskey, they could last as long as it took."[18]

Talking about the immensity of the ranch, Harvey admitted he did not see it all, but remembered the sounds and smells of nature, "The coyotes were singing on yonder Harvey Hill—that's its new name. I'd almost forgotten the twilight fragrance of Sycamore bark, but there it was again."[19]

In 2001, Herman began thinking about what would happen to the Diamond "H" Ranch. He decided that the Boy Scouts of America (BSA) would play a role in the ranch's future. For more than a decade, Herman had contributed to many Boy Scout projects, including the refurbishing of the offices of the Last Frontier Council of the BSA in Oklahoma City and the renovation of nearby Camp Kickapoo.[20]

Herman wanted Boy Scouts to learn to love and appreciate the outdoors—as he did. To provide a place for Scouts to do so, Herman and LaDonna agreed to give the ranch, in increments, to the Last Frontier Council of the Boy Scouts, beginning in 2005. The ranch will be known as the Diamond "H" Scout Ranch. Future plans include the construction of permanent facilities for use by Boy Scouts.

Facing page: **One of the most spectacular views on the ranch is from Lookout Point. From the cabin atop Red Spring Mountain, one can see Arkansas in the distance. Shaded by oak trees, visitors on the front porch of the cabin feel the constant breeze that blows across the prairie. The mountain is named for a spring that produces red-tinted water from the side of the mountain. The east side of the ranch adjoins a state-owned game preserve, Cookson Hills Game Refuge.**

Herman's sister, Linda Rice, second from right, daughter
Ashley, husband Con, and son Andrew. The Rice family
resides in Oklahoma City.

Herman patterned his gift after Oklahoma oil man
Waite Phillips, who contributed his New Mexico ranch to the
Boy Scouts in 1938. Philmont, a 215-square-mile national Boy
Scout camping area, is located in the rugged wilderness of the
Sangre de Cristo range of the Rocky Mountains.

After Phillips gave up personal ownership of his huge
ranch, he wrote a friend, "I hold that it is selfish to restrict the use
of anything like…Philmont to a small group like my own family
and personal friends when there is a wider opportunity for such
things to be enjoyed by the general public."[21] Herman and
LaDonna felt the same way.

As Boy Scouts in future generations come to the ranch
and learn the value of service to others and respect for the land,
a little bit of Herman's legacy will go with them as they become
adults and make valuable contributions to society. May everyone
who walks the hills and feels the breeze on the prairies of the
Diamond "H" Scout Ranch follow the dreams of Herman
Meinders.

Charley Kirk, a longtime
friend and fellow rancher,
has been a mentor to Herman
in operating the Diamond
"H" Ranch.

Endnotes

CHAPTER 1
GERMAN ROOTS

1 Interview with Glen Eichhorn, February 1, 2001, hereafter referred to as Glen Eichhorn interview, Heritage Archives, Oklahoma City, Oklahoma, hereafter referred to as Heritage Archives.
2 Interviews with Herman Meinders in April and May, 2004, hereafter referred to as Herman Meinders interview, Heritage Archives.
3 Ship brochure of the January 10, 1929 voyage on the Bremen, Heritage Archives.
4 www.germany-info.org
5 Ibid.
6 Herman Meinders interview.
7 www.pipestoneminnesota.com
8 Ibid.
9 Herman Meinders interview.
10 Glen Eichhorn interview.
11 Herman Meinders interview.
12 Interview with Arnold Janson, February 12, 2001.

CHAPTER 2
CHORES, CHORES, AND MORE CHORES

1 Herman Meinders interview.
2 Ibid.
3 Interview with George Schulze, February 19, 2001, hereafter referred to as George Schulze interview.
4 Herman Meinders interview.
5 Glen Eichhorn interview.

6 Interview with Donna Meinders Licquia, March 3, 2001, hereafter referred to as Donna Licquia interview.
7 Ibid.
8 Ibid.
9 Herman Meinders interview.
10 Interview with Jack Nessen, March 1, 2001, and April 23, 2004, hereafter referred to as Jack Nessen interview.
11 Herman Meinders interview.
12 Jack Nessen interview.
13 George Schulze interview.
14 Herman Meinders interview.
15 Interview with Denny Crook, October 6, 2001, hereafter referred to as Denny Crook interview.
16 Herman Meinders interview.
17 Ibid.
18 Ibid.
19 Ibid.

CHAPTER 3
FOLLOWING JACK

1 Herman Meinders interview.
2 Ibid.
3 Bob Burke and Kenny A. Franks, *Abe Lemons: Court Magician* (Oklahoma City: Oklahoma Heritage Association, 1999), p. 35.
4 Jack Nessen interview.
5 Herman Meinders interview.
6 Ibid.
7 Ibid.
8 Jack Nessen interview.
9 Herman Meinders interview.
10 Ibid.
11 Ibid.
12 Jack Nessen interview.
13 Herman Meinders interview.
14 Ibid.

15 Ibid.
16 Ibid.
17 Ibid.
18 Ibid.

CHAPTER 4
SAMMY'S BAR

1 Herman Meinders interview.
2 Ibid.
3 Ibid.
4 Jack Nessen interview.
5 Herman Meinders interview.
6 Ibid.
7 Ibid.
8 Ibid.
9 Ibid. and interview with Dale Murphy, March 12, 2001, hereafter referred to as Dale Murphy interview.
10 Ibid.
11 Herman Meinders interview.
12 Ibid.
13 Ibid., Dale Murphy interview.
14 Herman Meinders interview.
15 Ibid.
16 Ibid.
17 Ibid.
18 Ibid.
19 Ibid.
20 Dale Murphy interview.

CHAPTER 5
ON THE ROAD

1 Herman Meinders interview.
2 Barbara Grimes interview, March 10, 2001, hereafter referred to as Barbara Grimes interview.
3 Daniel J. Gilmartin, *Since 1910: A History of Florists' Transworld Delivery Association* (Southfield, Michigan, FTD Association, 1985),

p. v.
4 Ibid., p. vi.
5 www.ftd.com, the official website of Florists Transworld Delivery (FTD).
6 www.myteleflora.com, the official website of Teleflora.
7 Herman Meinders interview.
8 Ibid.
9 Ibid.
10 Interview with Ann Hobbs, March 29, 2001, Heritage Archives.
11 Dale Murphy interview.
12 Interview with Pete Garcia, March 29, 2001, hereafter referred to as Pete Garcia interview.
13 Herman Meinders interview.
14 Interview with Ken Benjamin, February 15, 2001, Heritage Archives.
15 Herman Meinders interview.
16 Ibid.
17 Ibid.
18 Ibid.
19 Ibid.
20 Barbara Grimes interview.
21 Herman Meinders interview.
22 Interview with Bill Plummer, March 1, 2001, hereafter referred to as Bill Plummer interview.
23 Interview with Bob Coleman, March 21, 2001, hereafter referred to as Bob Coleman interview.
24 Interview with Larry Hendershott, February 21, 2001, hereafter referred to as Larry Hendershott interview.
25 Ibid.
26 Jack Nessen interview.
27 Ibid.
28 Ibid.
29 Herman Meinders interview.

30 Ibid.

CHAPTER 6
FOUNDING A DREAM

1 Interview with Linda Meinders Rice, April 2, 2001, hereafter referred to as Linda Rice interview.
2 Ibid.
3 Herman Meinders interview.
4 Ibid.
5 Ibid.
6 Ibid.
7 Ibid.
8 Ibid.
9 Ibid.
10 Ibid.
11 Ibid.
12 Ibid.
13 Ibid.
14 Ibid.
15 Ibid.
16 Interview with LuCille Tudor, March 12, 2001, hereafter referred to as LuCille Tudor interview.
17 Herman Meinders interview.
18 Ibid.
19 LuCille Tudor interview.
20 Ibid.
21 Herman Meinders interview.
22 Ibid.
23 LuCille Tudor interview.

CHAPTER 7
STEADY GROWTH

1 Interview with Dean White, February 15, 2001, hereafter referred to as Dean White interview.
2 Interview with Jane Levieux, March 6, 2001, hereafter referred to as Jane Levieux interview.
3 Herman Meinders interview.
4 Ibid.

5 Ibid.
6 Ibid.
7 Interview with Basil Holt, February 10, 2001, hereafter referred to as Basil Holt interview.
8 Ibid.
9 Ibid.
10 Interview with Darrell Lake, March 6, 2001, Heritage Archives.
11 Ibid.
12 Herman Meinders interview.
13 Interview with Robert H. Meinders, February 18, 2001, hereafter referred to as Robert Meinders interview.
14 Herman Meinders interview.
15 Interview with Bill Winkler, May 14, 2004, Heritage Archives.
16 Undated copies of internal publications of AFS, Heritage Archives.
17 Ibid.
18 Robert Meinders interview.
19 Herman Meinders interview.
20 Basil Holt interview.
21 Ibid.
22 Ibid.
23 Interview with Walter Metz, March 10, 2001, hereafter referred to as Walter Metz interview.
24 Ibid.
25 Ibid.
26 Herman Meinders interview.
27 Interview with Robert "Bob" Newton, February 22, 2001, hereafter referred to as Robert Newton interview.
28 Ibid.

CHAPTER 8
GOOD TIMES AND DARK HOURS

1   Herman Meinders interview.
2   Letter from Donna Corjay to authors, June 10, 2004, Heritage Archives.
3   Interview with Johnny Childers, February 23, 2001, hereafter referred to as Johnny Childers interview.
4   Ibid.
5   Herman Meinders interview.
6   Ibid.
7   Ibid.
8   Ibid.
9   Ibid.
10 Ibid.
11 Ibid.
12 Interview with Steve Cassady, March 12, 2001, Heritage Archives.
13 Ibid.
14 Herman Meinders interview.
15 *Faces and Places,* Vol. 1, No. 1, February, 1981, Heritage Archives.
16 Interview with Herb Mitchell, January 15, 2001, hereafter referred to as Herb Mitchell interview.
17 *Faces and Places,* Vol. 1, No. 4, May, 1981, Heritage Archives.
18 Basil Holt interview.
19 Herman Meinders interview.
20 Basil Holt interview.
21 Herman Meinders interview.
22 Basil Holt interview.
23 Robert Meinders interview.
24 News release from files of American Floral Services, Heritage Archives, hereafter referred to as AFS news release; Interview with Jim Morley, February 21, 2001, hereafter referred to as Jim Morley interview.
25 Jim Morley interview.
26 Herb Mitchell interview.
27 Letter from Donna Corjay to authors, June 10, 2004, Heritage Archives.
28 Ibid.
29 Ibid.

CHAPTER 9
A NEW HOME OFFICE

1   Undated AFS promotional brochure, Heritage Archives.
2   Walter Metz interview.
3   Jim Morley interview.
4   Interview with Frances Dudley, February 16, 2001, hereafter referred to as Frances Dudley interview.
5   Interview with Katrina Holloway, February 16, 2001, Heritage Archives.
6   Ibid.
7   Herman Meinders interview.
8   Ibid.
9   Ibid.
10 Ibid.
11 Interview with Peter Moran, February 14, 2001, Heritage Archives.
12 Ibid.
13 Interview with Lynn Lary McLean, March 5, 2001, Heritage Archives.
14 Interview with Bob Carbone, April 16, 2001, Heritage Archives.
15 Herman Meinders interview.
16 Ibid.
17 *Faces and Places,* Vol. 2, No. 5, June, 1982, Heritage Archives.
18 Robert Meinders interview.
19 Interview with Mark Nance, March 6, 2001, Heritage Archives.
20 Interview with Paul Goodman, February 12, 2001, hereafter referred to as Paul Goodman interview.
21 Ibid.
22 Ibid.

CHAPTER 10
LETTING GO OF THE
REINS

1 Interview with Mildred Riddle, April 9, 2001, Heritage Archives.
2 AFS press release, October, 1985, Heritage Archives.
3 Interview with Tony Lovio, February 16, 2001, hereafter referred to as Tony Lovio interview.
4 Ibid.

CHAPTER 11
LADONNA

1 LaDonna Kramer Meinders, *Leaves In The Wind: A Celebration of Childhood in Rural Oklahoma* (Inola, Oklahoma: Evans Publications, Inc., 1989), p. 17, hereafter referred to as *Leaves In The Wind.*
2 Ibid., p. viii.
3 Ibid.
4 Ibid., p. 7.
5 Ibid., p. 9.
6 Ibid., p. 22.
7 Ibid., p. 24.
8 Ibid., p. 49; Interview with Ruth Evelyn Kramer Seideman, February 17, 2001, hereafter referred to as Ruth Seideman interview.
9 *Leaves In The Wind*, p. 69.
10 Ibid., p. 126.
11 Ibid., p. 127.
12 Ibid., p. 136.
13 Ibid., p. 139.
14 Interview with LaDonna Jane Kramer Meinders, May 20, 2004, hereafter referred to as LaDonna Meinders interview.
15 Ibid.
16 Jim Morley interview.
17 LaDonna Meinders interview.
18 Ibid.
19 Ibid.
20 Ibid.

CHAPTER 12
THE MILLION DOLLAR
CONVENTION

1 Johnny Childers interview.
2 Interview with Dan Curtin, January 29, 2001, hereafter referred to as Dan Curtin interview.
3 Ibid.
4 Robert Meinders interview.
5 Tony Lovio interview.
6 Interview with Jimmie Jarrell, March 10, 2001, hereafter referred to as Jimmie Jarrell interview.
7 Ibid.
8 Ibid.
9 Dan Curtin interview.
10 Frances Dudley interview

CHAPTER 13
SELLING THE BUSINESS

1 Offering Memorandum, Cruttenden & Company, 1993, prepared for the sale of American Floral Services, Inc., hereafter referred to as Cruttenden & Company Offering Memorandum.
2 Herman Meinders interview.
3 Cruttenden & Company Offering Memorandum.
4 Ibid.
5 Ibid.
6 Ibid.
7 Ibid.
8 Interview with Mo Grotjohn, April 20, 2004, hereafter referred to as Mo Grotjohn interview.
9 Ibid.

10 Ibid.
11 Ibid.
12 Ibid.
13 Ibid.
14 Ibid.
15 Ibid.
16 Ibid.
17 Ibid.
18 Ibid.
19 Ibid.
20 Interview with Gregg Coccari, March 21, 2001, hereafter referred to as Gregg Coccari interview.

CHAPTER 14
A CHARITABLE HEART

1 Mo Grotjohn interview.
2 Ibid.
3 Herman Meinders interview.
4 Interview with Ray Ackerman, May 1, 2004, Heritage Archives.
5 Interview with Vince Orza, April 10, 2001, Heritage Archives.
6 Interview with Ron Norick, April 9, 2001, Heritage Archives.
7 Linda Rice interview.
8 Pete Garcia interview.
9 Interview with Steve Martinez, February 14, 2001, Heritage Archives.
10 Financial records of the Meinders Foundation, Heritage Archives.
11 Ibid.
12 Ibid.
13 Ibid.
14 George Schulze interview.
15 Ibid.
16 Ibid.
17 Mo Grotjohn interview.
18 Ibid.
19 Interview with Tom McDaniel, April 13, 2004, Heritage Archives.

20 Mo Grotjohn interview.
21 Interview with Bishop Bruce Blake, April 21, 2001, Heritage

CHAPTER 15
HOME ON THE RANGE: THE DIAMOND "H" RANCH

1 Bruce Joseph and Bob Burke, *A Guide to Oklahoma's Historical Markers* (Oklahoma City: Oklahoma Historical Society, 2004), pre-publication manuscript, p. 27.
2 Herman Meinders interview.
3 Ibid.
4 Tony Lovio interview.
5 Ibid.
6 Ibid.
7 Interview with Scott Edwards, April 9, 2001, Heritage Archives.
8 Interview with Peggy Bishop, March 19, 2001, Heritage Archives.
9 Interview with Ken Freytag, March 6, 2001, Heritage Archives.
10 Ibid.
11 Jim Morley interview.
12 Dean White interview.
13 LaDonna Meinders interview.
14 Ibid.
15 Herman Meinders interview.
16 Ibid.
17 Transcript of Paul Harvey News, ABC Radio Network, November 8, 1993, Heritage Archives.
18 Ibid.
19 Ibid.
20 Interview with Paul Moore, April 16, 2001, hereafter referred to as Paul Moore interview.
21 Letter from Waite Phillips to Walter Head, March 16, 1945, Heritage Archives.

Index

Oahu, HI 62
Ode, Alexandra 137-138, 143
Ode, Chris 137
Ode, Craig 132, 137-138, 143
Ode, Lori Gooden 137
O'Fallon, MO 171
Ohio 17, 49-50, 56, 154
Ojibwa 18
Okeene,130
Oklahoma viii, 37, 39, 97-98, 129, 133, 136-137, 142, 181, 183-184, 189, 191, 197, 203
Oklahoma Arts Council 136
Oklahoma Centennial 2007 184
Oklahoma Christian University 183
Oklahoma City 37-38, 41, 54, 59, 65, 67-69, 72, 76, 82-83, 88, 90, 93-95 , 100-101, 113, 116, 124, 128, 135, 141, 143-144, 152-153, 155-156, 163-168, 170, 181, 183, 185, 187, 190, 197, 205; Oklahoma County 111, 179
Oklahoma City Museum of Art 183
Oklahoma City Philharmonic 183
Oklahoma City Police Department 93
Oklahoma City University (OCU) 37, 38, 39, 40, 136, 139, 140, 141, 143, 174, 176, 179, 181, 183, 185, 186, 187, 188, 189, 190, 199, 201; School of Music 136
Oklahoma Council of Public Affairs 183
Oklahoma Department of Wildlife Conservation 202
Oklahoma Educational Television Authority 183
Oklahoma Hall of Fame 178
Oklahoma Heritage Association viii, 178, 183-184
Oklahoma Territory 37
Oklahoma City YMCA 184
Oklahoma Department of Libraries viii
Oklahoma Historical Society viii, 184
Oklahoma Publishing Company viii, 134, 182
Oklahoma School of Science and Mathematics 183

Oklahoma State Capitol 184-185
Oklahoma State University 183
Oklahoma Territory 129
Olathe, KS 64
Omnimax Theatre 149
Omniplex 183
Order of Achievement 180
Order of Merit 180
Orlando, FL 156-159
Orza, Vince 179-180
Oscars 156
Oto 18
Overmeyer, Bob 89, 92, 113
Overmeyer, Eulalah 89, 92, 94, 99, 102, 113, 158
P
Pacific Ocean 61
Padilla, Mary 40
Palatine, IL 129
Pan O'Gold Bakery 26
Pan Pacific Flower Culture Conference 118-119
Pape, Ken 36
Paragould, AR 170
Park Hill 192
Patnaude, Sandra 83
Patrick Henry College 183
Pawnee 18
Peak, Connie vii
Pennock, Charles 182
Pennsylvania 17, 196
Perimeter Center 170
Pete Garcia Company 92
Petuskey, Tom 111
Phillips Theological Seminary 184
Phillips, Waite 206
Philmont 206
Phoenix, AZ 63
Phillippines 119
Phillips, Mary viii
Picayune, Mississippi 150-151
Pierret, Jerome 36
Pipestone, MN 15, 17-19, 22, 24, 26, 28-30, 33-35, 38, 43-45, 63-65, 79, 116, 141, 175, 184; Pipestone County 18, 45

Meinders School of Business
Oklahoma City University